How to Capture
a Mistress

First Edition

Karen Martin

How to Capture a Mistress

First Edition

Published by The Nazca Plains Corporation
Las Vegas, Nevada
2006

ISBN: 978-1-887895-75-0

Published by

The Nazca Plains Corporation ®
4640 Paradise Rd, Suite 141
Las Vegas, NV 89109-8000

Cover Photo by Corwin
Art Direction Blake Stephens

Dedication

This book is dedicated to my slave, Robert J. Rubel, who – despite my best efforts – managed to capture me.

Acknowledgements

First and foremost, I want to thank Master Robert Steele and my slave, Robert J. Rubel, for pushing me not only to write this book, but also to keep working on it and to get it finished. I don't usually write non-fiction, and this was a challenge. I also thank Corwin for shooting the cover photo and the portrait of slave Robert Rubel and me. On this same topic, I thank my slave's slave, mindi, for making the final line edits. Clearly, this book would not have been written without everyone's help.

How to Capture a Mistress

Karen Martin

Contents

Appendices:

Introduction

Why did I write this book? I wrote this book out of frustration. Men who have incredible needs write to me offering service, financial domination, relocation to places I have no interest in visiting, and long-term relationships usually by the second e-mail exchange, not understanding that what they have to offer is not what I need or want. Their approach is similar to bulk mailing. Men write many, many women in hopes of finding their one true mate, a Dominant lady who will fulfill their fantasies.

In writing this book, I believe a gentleman of quality will be able to pursue the dream of capturing a Dominant Lady and begin another chapter in the "Happily Ever After" of their kinky lives. The gentleman has to rethink how he is going to pursue her. Because this book was written for males who wish to form healthy relationships with FemDoms, the gender throughout the book will be male submissive, Female Dominant.

Every male deserves a Mistress even if he hasn't had much luck finding one. He just may be looking for the wrong things in the wrong places. He may not be looking at all, assuming she will find him. Or, he may be wounded from a perfect relationship that suddenly soured. None of this matters as of this reading because it is in the past, and all we have is now.

It's a journey, and a new day is upon us.

An M/s Studies Book

Chapter One
The Basics of Kinky Play

Kink and Non-Kink

It is important, whether in this book or any other BDSM book, to have a solid understanding of kink and non-kink behaviors. Non-kink is the way you live when you want to blend into the majority of social situations, such as Thanksgiving dinner and office parties. Kink is the way your mind thinks, the secrets you keep from friends and family and the twisted way you get pleasure from thoughts and activities that might appall most people if they knew. You may actually perform these acts, or they may be living in exile in your fantasies. Consider the possibility that perhaps others are as kinky as you and don't reveal it for fear of your rejection.

> ** Hot Tip: Don't confide in people who haven't revealed to you that they are kinky or kink friendly.*

Unfortunately, when we think we've found the perfect someone to complete our less-than-happy lives, or we have another revelation about our kinky selves, we often make the mistake of letting other vanilla (non-kink) people in on the secret. Most of the time, this is a lousy idea and will come back to bite us in ways that hadn't occurred to us when we confided in the wrong person about the right kink.

How do you know when to share your kinky proclivities and aspirations with others? Let them know about it when they bring it up to you. They have either caught a few of the nonverbal signals, or they recognize what you and the Lady you are pursuing are doing. Either way, let them be the ones to broach the "K" word.

Kinky Play

Beware of Checklists

One way to pursue a Dominant Lady is to find common ground with her kinks and yours. There are as many kinks and play styles out there as there are people to embrace them. Rather than present the standard checklist with numerous columns for preferences and willingness to play, we are going to explore categories of kinky activities. I have found that when prospective play partners become too specific as to the type of activity preferred, the play may not occur at all because it appears there is no connection or common ground. The areas of interest in play become so vastly disparate that a match cannot be found. Both the FemDom and male submissive walk away unfulfilled.

To clarify this disparity, pretend you wanted to share an entrée with a hot date at a Chinese restaurant. You wouldn't say, "I am only interested in ordering a Pu-Pu Platter, sizzling rice soup, #47 Kung Pao Shrimp with a hot and spicy rating of 3, steamed rice, and jasmine tea as served by Liu in the third booth to the left of the Buddha which is closest to the air conditioner. Although I prefer standard linen table service, I would tolerate chopsticks, but only if you absolutely insist. Take-out is a hard no, because I had a bad experience with a phone order in 2001. So, what do you like?"

Of course you wouldn't say that. Who would go out with you more than once? Who would share a meal with you at all? However, that is precisely the modus operandi when we use analytical checklists to specify our wants, rather than find common ground based on our needs. Because checklists are readily available on the internet and touted as "the thing to do," we assume they are adequate.

Here is an abridged example of my own making.

BDSM CHECKLIST

Kinky Activity	Experienced? Yes/No	Willingness? No...0-5...Yes
Anal plug, large		
Animal play, pony		
Beating, soft		

In my experience, a BDSM activity checklist is simply a list of possible activities and should be viewed without judgment, especially when we have not actually participated in nor viewed the activity upon which we are supposed to determine not only our preference, but also whether or not we'd like to try it at some point in our lives with someone we may not yet have met.

In our vanilla lives, it would be like giving you a list of dance forms and asking you to rate your preferences as a beginning dance student. Do you recognize the Argentine Tango from any other kind? Probably not, so how would you be able to make a decision with any degree of validity? You can't, nor would you.

The same is true of BDSM checklists. As a personal faux pas, I listed "Rough Sex" as a preference when I was a novice. I liked to wrestle and then surrender, so I felt rough sex was a pretty good description, given the Internet checklist I was using. Some of you are smiling at this moment. When I actually witnessed two gay gentlemen having what is commonly referred to by them as rough sex, I realized how I had almost put myself in jeopardy by asking for something I did not understand.

However, had I used "rough sex" as a springboard to communication, which is probably how the checklists were intended to be used, I would have rapidly erased that checkmark.

BDSM checklists have the added disadvantage of usually being listed in alphabetical order. Beware of falling prey to the halo effect. That's when you find the absolutely best activity in the world in the letter "S", and you are so enrapt that you don't write down "Sex with Snakes" as a hard no. The reverse may also be true. You find an activity in the "H" list that is abhorrent and then do not rate highly enough a perfectly acceptable activity that is listed immediately after the one that turned your stomach.

Another problem occurs when you have not rated highly enough one of the strongly desired activities requested by the FemDom. By experimenting with kinky play that had not made it into your original fantasies, you may later be able to negotiate for the style of play that meets your wants.

Common sense and experience tell us that we know better than to specify so minutely what we will and will not tolerate if the goal is to have a mutually fulfilling experience, especially with a new partner. We negotiate. We get our needs met and hopefully, as many of our wants as possible. We get into the spirit of cooperation, resulting in a synergy we could not have experienced had we dined or played alone.

The same is true for kinky play. The typical Internet checklists restrict our open minds and narrow the possible play partners until there aren't many, and we're alone.

Redefine Kink

If you view kink activities in categories, rather than as specific activities, it opens you to communicate with the FemDoms and promotes a flexible approach that is more conducive to playing.

For the purpose of this text, kinky play activities are divided into the following forms of play: Bondage, Impact, Sensory, Intense, Genital, Insertion, Fetish and Bodily Fluid. I chose these categories because they make sense to me. If they don't make sense to you, alter them. Otherwise, try to accept this structure, because it should present more opportunities to get play partners. Having play partners may lead to relationships beyond the one-night-stand, should that be your goal.

Most people I have interviewed have a favorite kink. If you aren't certain of yours, review all of the things that make you want to masturbate. That list can be a basis for selecting kinky play activities. The broader your list, the greater the opportunity there will be to play.

Some activities can easily be included in more than one category. For negotiation purposes, it behooves you to find ways that your kinks can survive in more than one category. For example, if your Dominant Lass likes bondage, and you want to sleep in a chastity device, it's better if you view this activity as Bondage Play, rather than rigidly relegating it to Genital Play. If your nipples are very sensitive, nipple clamps may be considered Intense Play. If your nipples can really take a lot of punishment, you may feel most nipple play is Sensual play. The better you communicate, the more likely you will have satisfying play experiences.

The following bulleted lists are comprised of suggested activities for separate categories of play and they are to be used primarily as tools during the introductory stages of negotiation with a prospective partner. Your play style may indicate that some activities are better served in another category. In each category, there is an activity marked "Other", because you may not see your passion listed, and it deserves to have a space where you feel it fits best.

I define Bondage Play as a desire for physical restriction or the desire to physically restrict others. If you like to be restricted in your movement and ability to free yourself, you may consider bondage as a common interest with a FemDom. We'll discuss the power play aspects in the next section. This is physical, and what you like being done to you, and what you will tolerate doing to please that Dominant Lady of your Dreams.

> ** Hot Tip: Some FemDoms like to be on the receiving end. It is a real coup when a submissive male is chosen to serve her in this way.*

Bondage Play
- Content (metal, leather, Saran Wrap™, rope, etc.)
- Use (chastity, suspension, mummification, corset, harness, gag, etc.)
- Level of restriction (stocks, sleep sack, straight jacket, etc.)
- Other

If your fantasies surround being struck, or if you can wrap your head around striking others, you may be interested in Impact Play. Choose the activity and not the power exchange that surrounds it. That is covered in the next section.

Some of you are masochists and like the idea or the act of being slapped, hit or struck. Some of you enjoy being teased, and some of you crave the scenario that surrounds the play activity. Choose the kink activity and save the power exchange scenario for later.

Impact Play
- Designed for striking (paddle, strap, crop, flogger, whip, etc.)
- Not originally designed for striking (hairbrush, wooden spoon, etc. - also known as "pervertables".)
- Body part (hand, fist for striking, foot for kicking, etc.)
- Other

You already know the five senses: touch, smell, sight, hearing, and taste. If your fantasies are enhanced by either the stimulation or the deprivation of experiencing an activity through your senses, you may enjoy Sensory Play.

Sensory Play
- Sensory Deprivation (blindfolds, ear plugs, gags, etc.)
- Sensory Enhancement (tickling, massage, aromas, videos, music)
- Sensory Toys
  1. Abrasion toys (talons, vampire gloves, feathers, shaving, knives, etc.)
  2. Temperature toys (ice, hot oil, air, etc.)
  3. Pinch toys (clothespins, clamps, nipple clamps, etc.)
  4. Food as a toy (eating, tasting, smelling, etc.)
  5. Music or sounds to set the mood or manipulate a scene
  6. Scents (candles, oils, etc.)
  7. Visual toys (videos, photos, etc.)
  8. Other

If you fantasize about the more extreme activities, you may desire Intense Play. These forms of play require personal mentoring to master and do not translate well to the skills of the novice FemDom.

Intense Play
- Electricity (TENS, cattle prod, violet wand, etc.)
- Heat or Fire Play (branding, hot wax, devil's fire, alcohol play, etc.)
- Breath Play (I don't recommend this one; it scares me)
- Other

If you fantasize about playing with your privates - or even better, playing with hers, Genital Play may be for you. Each of you needs your own personal toys, and you need to know how to keep them clean.

Genital Play
- Sex (fellatio, cunnilingus, rimming, penetration, hand job)
- Vibrator play
- Cock and Ball torture/Pussy torture
- Other

If you eroticize the action of something entering you, Insertion Play may be a kink that has your name on it. You may wish to enter the Lady, but it is her prerogative to decide whether or not your desires match hers.

Insertion Play
- Anal (penetration sex, plug, speculum, food, dildo, strap-on, fisting, etc.)
- Vaginal (see above)
- Urethral (sounds)
- Any other orifice (an opening in the body)

Now, I am a fetishist. I adore it and could speak about it for hours. We love the "thing." We fantasize the nouns. It is extremely important to us that the clothing or body part look right, feel right, taste right, etc. Add the power exchange dynamic, which is discussed in the next section, and you have the beginnings of a fascinating evening together.

Fetish Play
- Constitution of clothing (leather, rubber, latex, nylon, etc.)
- Type of clothing (corset, shoe, boot, lingerie, etc.)
- Body part (foot, breast, bottom, etc.)
- Occasion (cross dressing, gender play, public play, using any of the above in a scene)

Then there is that group of perverted pals whom I adore, the ones whose own bodily fluids, or the fluids of that special Lady, become erotic. Because of the dangers of spreading disease and infection, we need to take special care when playing with bodily fluids. It is the responsibility of the male, as well as the FemDom, to protect the union and ensure that stringent safety procedures be followed.

Bodily Fluids Play
- Urine (golden showers, swallowing, chamber pot use, etc.)
- Feces (enemas, brown showers, scat play, diapers, etc.)
- Blood (cutting, needle play, piercing, scarification, etc.)
- Other bodily fluids (saliva, etc.)

Conclusion
At this point, you are separating your kink from your non-kink play preferences. You are less likely to fall prey to the widespread practice of using an activity checklist before knowing either the FemDom you are playing with or experiencing a style of play that may be new to you. You can sort kinky play into eight broad categories and have a concept of what each one entails. You have identified what kinky play you would like to explore and have attempted to attach it to more than one category so that you will have a maximum number of play partners. Most importantly, you are expanding your tolerance and acceptance of others, even if their kinks do not match yours.

Now, it is time to explore the fascinating dynamics of power exchange, which is crucial to capturing a Mistress.

Chapter Two
The Basics of Playing with Power

Power Exchange

Power exchange is the synergy that happens when a male voluntarily gifts a Lady with the privilege of directing him and guiding him during their time together. The power exchange is complete when the Lady accepts responsibility for the welfare and direction of the petitioning (requesting) male. The power exchange may be for an evening, a lifetime, or any time in between.

Power exchange has its own set of dynamics that are complementary to the kinky activities in the last section. Choose your kink. Then select your level of power exchange. Embrace the possibilities and ignore the negative self-talk that sounds like, "This won't work. Who would want to do that with me?"

For an activity such as rope bondage, you may wish to be the captured soldier or simply a bondage demo bottom with little or no power exchange taking place. For the cane and switch, you may wish to be the young lad who has stolen a pear from Ms. Brenna's prized pear tree. Select the kink activities that appeal to you, and then figure out the level of power exchange you need to create a memorable experience.

For some gentlemen, the power exchange is vastly more important than the kinky activity. In that case, it is more important to select the level of power exchange before matching it to the kink activity. For example, if the FemDom is into paddles and straps, and the bottom is into strict disciplinary power exchanges, there is a good opportunity for a play match.

There are as many types of power exchange as there are couples or groups to enact them. For the purposes of this book, we are going to consider power exchange as Service, Persona, Discipline, Humiliation, Restriction, Conquest and Forced Play.

Service Play is a marvelous opportunity for the male to serve and the

FemDom to receive. These activities translate well to 24/7 relationships or long-term relationships. In service, we can always be in a scene. On the other hand, we can play for only a few hours. Both are perfect.

Service play is very attractive to a FemDom, and she may invite a gent into her dungeon who would otherwise not make it through her filters. Make a list of skills you have that your new Mistress can use. Don't add value to them, just make the list. It is her decision as to how valuable those skills are to her, and you may never even know which one you possess that she desires most.

Service Play
- Sexual (phone sex, pleasing Ma'am in any sexual way she specifies, toy boy, sissy time, etc.)
- Personal (grooming, following orders, anticipating her needs, errand boy, personal assistant, etc.)
- Household (chauffeur, butler, chef, pool boy, handyman, etc.)
- Community (serving as a volunteer, facilitating Mistress when she volunteers, acting as a safe call, fundraising, acting as a mentor, giving presentations, etc.)
- Other

The Lovely Lady is hosting a Sunday brunch with three of her friends, but she falls behind in preparations. You come to her aid when she allows you to do the last minute grocery shopping, vacuum the carpet, and set the table, which impresses her no end that you know how. Then you surprise her with fresh flowers which you arrange in a centerpiece. You have followed directions, but just as importantly, thought ahead and acted in her best interest, making her table more attractive for her guests. As you are leaving, you offer to act as valet and park the cars for the ladies, knowing that apartment parking is at a premium. She takes you up on the offer and somehow you end up serving all four ladies who do not hesitate to tell the Lovely Lady how lucky she is to have you.

If you actually dress up and assume the role of the maid or the butler, it becomes Persona Play.

Persona Play is the "pretend" playground that we enter into when we want to take or relinquish control with a special someone. This is the consummate role play that sends us into fantasies extraordinaire. It is separated by lifestyle long-term Restriction Play and Conquest Play, because it is primarily scene related for short durations. The emphasis is on the creation of the scene, not on obedience, submission or surrender, although they may be elements of the scene.

For example, you may enjoy age play in which you are nurtured, guided and disciplined by a matronly female you call "Auntie." It is persona play, because it is of short duration. Although you may always view her as "Auntie", there are times when you have to act like the vibrant, dynamic, powerful adult you are. The same goes for other styles of Persona Play. If you can't live 24/7 in the role of pony or patient or pupil, you're in Persona Play.

You may have fantasized about being the worthless, naked, chained slave prostrate at the Amazon's feet. She's in charge; you aren't. When you mess up, she'll punish you in ways you've pre-negotiated. She may turn you into a pony and use that horse hair butt plug you presented to her last week.

Persona Play
- Age play (governess/pupil, Mommy/baby, Auntie/boy)
- Animal play (kitty, puppy, pony, etc.)
- Ownership play (temporary collars, slave auctions, etc.)
- Scenario play (religious, schoolroom, medical, prison, etc.)
- Other

Not all Persona Play has elements of discipline. Sometimes, it's a nurturing, playful relationship between a Trainer and her new puppy. Sometimes, it's a reward for a temporary slave who wants a special kind of treat. She's still in charge, but it is a celebration and a time to be cherished, not a discipline scenario in which the gent has been caught misbehaving. Dealing with that misbehavior is still Persona Play because it is of short duration and carried out in a role that could not be maintained permanently, day in and day out.

If you want long-term, 24/7, you may be interested in Discipline Play. Discipline Play, as it is used in this context, is similar to Persona Play because both forms of play involve authority exchange. In Discipline Play, however, the scene is designed to be a long-term arrangement, perhaps even for a lifetime. Think of them as kinky marriage vows. They last. Yes, Discipline Play is fluid and can be altered as needed, but essentially, it is a constitution for the relationship and is not short term, scene-based play as is Persona Play.

Discipline Play
- Physical (carrot/stick reward and punishment systems, penance, rituals, protocols, etc.)
- Mental (lectures for misbehavior, rules of the household, remediation of personal character flaws, etc.)
- Other

For example, Jane takes her lover John in hand when she finds out his job is threatened, because he is repeatedly late for work. She announces that he is to be punished for his poor work ethic. That evening, wearing a corset, girdle and gartered stockings, she guides him over her lap for a traditional hairbrush spanking. Every Friday until New Year's he will present his time card to her, and she will either discipline him or reward him as needed. It's Discipline Play, because the most important element is the discipline, not the role the participants are playing. In addition, the structure can last a lifetime. As a side benefit, the kinky relationship is not obvious to others.

At times, the Discipline Play will accelerate to being Humiliation Play, usually for repeated transgressions or to emphasize the seriousness of a poor choice made on the part of the gentleman who, lacking self discipline, must rely on his Lady to keep him in line. Humiliation Play is usually of short duration if it is to be effective over the long haul.

Humiliation Play is that extraordinarily erotic form of risky play common in FemDom/male submissive relationships. These are primarily scene related, highly negotiated, and do not necessarily translate well for long periods of time. Humiliation Play pairs nicely with Service Play and Persona Play.

Humiliation Play
- Physical (corner time, diaper play, exposure to others, wearing of clothing, sissy play, cuckold scenario, etc.)
- Mental (castration fantasy, fear, verbal threats/descriptions, small penis play, guilt, etc.)
- Other

For example, the gentleman has not completed a list of weekly chores, nor has he notified the Lady that the tasks would not be completed to specification or deadline. Therefore, it is a violation of Service Play. She assumes the role of Mistress, forces her lover to wear a sissy maid outfit and belittles him as he strives to complete the chores correctly.

Make note that the same sissy maid outfit could be a reward and cherished role for one gent, but a humiliation and punishment for another. The costume is the same. The chores are the same. The difference is in the perspective of the gentleman. If part of his kink is a need for humiliation, then the sissy maid costume is humiliating. If he revels in his feminine role in the household, being allowed to wear the sissy maid costume is a reward and celebration of his service, which would not be Humiliation Play. It would be a combination of Service Play and Persona Play.

Many men have confused the practice of being humiliated with the desire. If part of the masturbation fantasy is humiliation, it is Humiliation Play. If the erotic fantasy has nothing to do with humiliation, but the man assumes he has to be humiliated to get his needs met, it is a miscommunication that can lead to abuse.

For example, one of my playmates was a gorgeous young man who had a leg and stocking fetish. He was busily groveling and begging to serve, but it didn't appear to me that his heart was in it. When I allowed him to prepare my lingerie and put on my stockings, it became obvious that this was the kink that made him ecstatic. He had incorrectly assumed that he would have to be humiliated before he would be allowed to worship the stockings.

The next time we met, I had lined up several ladies, not all of whom were dominant, but who were all wearing his preferred style of pantyhose. In one evening, he learned that he did not need Humiliation Play at all, nor was he likely to invite it into a session.

The opposite was true when a gentleman was constantly misbehaving on purpose. I assumed it was Persona Play inviting punishment, and we began to play. The scene didn't work. Afterward, over coffee, I asked him to describe a scene that would have worked. Given the number of slights and the severity of the remarks he wanted me to make, I suggested that next time he negotiate Humiliation Play up front, rather than hoping the FemDom would stumble into that territory by accident when he had angered her. In other words, it would not have occurred to me to criticize the size of his penis since we weren't doing anything with it during the scene. In addition, I don't normally tromp on the thin ice of a man's ego unless asked. Do not expect a Lady to use Humiliation Play without negotiating for it up front. In addition, she may not agree to it until she is comfortable with you as a kinky play partner.

Humiliation may not have your name on it. However, you may enjoy giving over control for a short time or even longer. Therefore, consider Restriction Play, Forced Play and Conquest Play as forms to negotiate.

Restriction Play is a power exchange in which the authority figure has decided the bottom will not engage in or will restrict how or if a certain activity is performed for a given length of time. In objectification, the restriction is made that the bottom is no longer functioning as a human, but serves as the object Ma'am needs. Restriction Play can be used for a lengthy duration when coupled with a set of behaviors that are used when vanilla folks are present. Obedience is important in Restriction Play.

Restriction Play
- Sexual (orgasm control, orgasm denial, etc.)
- Retention (enema, speech restrictions, bathroom use, etc.)
- Physical (speech, sleep, weight control, use of furniture, etc.)
- Objectification (foot stool, toilet, ashtray, art, etc.)
- Other

For example, in a long-term Mistress/slave power exchange, the gentleman may not be allowed to use furniture, or to speak, or he may have to address his Mistress in a particular manner, may serve as her footstool, and may not touch her without permission. The self discipline that is required of the man is evidenced as the gift of obedience. The scene may take place every evening that they are alone. The male slave in this particular scenario, however, must feel fulfilled through acts of obedience, must enjoy silence, and must revel in being treated as an object.

If he doesn't enjoy any of those things, he is inviting abuse through his own lack of communication or negotiating skills. Because Restriction Play requires the endorsement of both parties, it is easily negotiable. If you enjoy Restriction Play, but need the feeling of having to do it against your will, you may desire Forced Play.

Forced Play takes Restriction Play to a new level because the male is no longer perceived as giving permission to the FemDom to act on his behalf. There is the illusion of the FemDom making or forcing the gentleman to participate in activities he would not have chosen for himself. Obedience and submission are necessary for Forced Play.

Forced Play
- Sexual (masturbation, nudity, exercise, etc.)
- Activity based (weight loss or gain, exercise, nudity, etc.)
- Object based (chosen food, chosen clothing, etc,)
- Other

For example, Lovely Lady owns you. You have mastered the art and craft of obedience, and she is pleased. If both parties are fulfilled, it is difficult to maintain the excitement, and life becomes routine. Therefore, she adds an element of Forced Play you wrote to her about several months ago involving forced masturbation. Knowing you fear being exposed in public, she takes it to the next level and commandeers the steam bath in your apartment complex. Armed with a timer and a digital camera, she directs your activity until you climax and then makes you watch the video clip. She isn't humiliating you, but she is demanding more from you than obedience.

If this play turns you on, and you want to explore further the erotic sensations of being forced to do an activity you would not normally choose for yourself, consider Conquest Play.

* Hot tip: Only engage in Conquest Play with FemDoms who come with strong references or those with whom you have solid relationships.

Conquest play is when the aggressor, or FemDom, captures the unfortunate slave who doesn't seem to take advantage of the opportunities to escape. Obedience, submission and surrender are elements of Conquest Play. The male must convince himself he is truly under her control and could not escape despite obvious evidence to the contrary.

Conquest Play
- Short term (wrestling, kidnapping, faux rape, slave competitions, etc.)
- Long-term (training or permanent collars, rituals, ceremonies of affection or ownership such as piercing, branding, or body art, etc.)
- Mental (hypnotism, ownership, fear, etc.)
- Other

For example, both the FemDom and the male enjoy medical scenes. Through extensive negotiation, the Mad Scientist kidnaps the unwilling specimen, secures him to the dentist's chair in her dungeon, and injects saline solutions that increase his ball size by half. It's Persona Play, because she's a Mad Scientist and he's a subject in the experiment, but it has the focus that the play is not consensual, and that the Mad Scientist is more interested in the results of the experiment than in the welfare of the captured test subject.

Many of the activities we engage in during Restriction Play can also be utilized in Forced Play. In Restriction Play, the male chooses to obey willingly. In Forced Play, there is the added layer of illusion that if given a choice, the male would not have made the same choice as his did his Mistress.

For example, Persona Play, Restriction Play and Forced Play can be combined to create a marvelous afternoon between the wicked stiletto-heeled nurse and her unfortunate straight-jacketed patient. Persona Play is the nurse/patient dynamic. Restriction play includes the straight jacket, and Forced Play is when she pulls out the enema equipment and there isn't much he can do about it. She nurtures him and cajoles him into asking for the enema. He wants to please her and decides to obey even though he makes it clear he's only doing it for her, which she believes until he has an erection the size of the Washington Monument. This scene is vastly different from the Conquest scene described before it.

Forced Play must be differentiated from Conquest play. Conquest Play is Forced Play with the added layer of illusion that that the bottom has no choice and is powerless to avoid what Ma'am has decided. In Forced Play, the Lady has the male's best interests in mind. In Conquest Play, she is devoted to the role she plays and the problem to be solved in the situation, giving the illusion that his safety and welfare are inconsequential or even forfeit.

For example, in an interrogation scene, which is primarily Conquest Play, the uniformed Captain has bound her unfortunate spy to a chair, legs spread apart, privates exposed. She's hidden the bandage scissors and any-thing else that would indicate to the prisoner that she has his best interests in mind. The gag may be a bit larger than what he's used to. It is only removed when she asks a question, and her next step is based upon his answer. Yes, he is controlling the scene with his responses, including telling her what she wants to know, but she is free to strike fear in his heart and balls.

One style of play may or may not be more extreme than the others. It is in the perception of the bottom whether the agreed upon activity is defined as Restriction Play, Forced Play or Conquest Play.

The actions of the FemDom remain within the negotiated constructs of the style of play. She has an obligation to keep the activities in the scene within the play style to which the male has agreed. Problems occur when the man thinks he's in a Restriction scene because he likes the idea of pretending to be an end table, but the Mistress has not perceived his request and moves into a Conquest scene in which not only is he a table, but he is used to serve a three-course dinner and learns that he'll have to wear a diaper because she's not letting him up until midnight. Because he is a table, he can't speak; there-fore, he has no safe words to stop or slow the scene. He can't move, so he has no safe word movements. His options are to simply stop serving, which can be devastating to his self-esteem, or he can endure. Either way, he is not living his dream, and indeed, may never want to be a table again. The Top has no idea what went wrong, because all she did was what he had asked. It gets worse if we have a mouthy submissive male who tells everyone he knows what a rotten FemDom she was and that she is probably dangerous.

That is perhaps an exaggeration, but it emphasizes the necessity of open communication during negotiations, to insure a safe and fulfilling scene.

Differences in three forms of power play
- Restriction - obedience
- Forced - obedience and submission
- Conquest - obedience, submission and surrender

The same kinky activity can have three different levels of power exchange. For example, use of a chastity device could be viewed as simple Restriction Play by one man who gets joy out of being obedient to the Lady, who told him to buy it, put it on when she calls and leave the key in his pocket. It may feel Forced to the gentleman who would never have worn the device if Mistress hadn't put it on him and insisted he must ask permission to remove it. It could be considered Conquest if the chastity device was put on during a kidnapping scene. She has the key, and he has been forbidden to cut the plastic band unless he has a medical emergency.

In addition, any of the above forms of play can be combined with Service, Persona, Discipline or Humiliation Play. It is less important to pigeonhole the activity and power exchange than it is to create a mutually fulfilling experience in which both parties understand and consent.

In preparation to meet a Lovely Lady of Dominance, you have learned to identify levels and styles of kinky play and power exchange that are fulfilling to you. You clearly understand the need to negotiate and communicate clearly with a prospective play partner. Perhaps you are more open to considering a variety of play partners, styles and play than you were when you read the first page of this book. The more versatile you are, the more opportunities you will see, and the more chances you have to play. The more you play and are seen playing, the greater the odds of finding a Lady who fulfills your wants and needs.

Pitfalls of Power Exchange

At this point, it behooves me to insert a few warnings. It's time to develop a filter to screen out kinky activities, levels of power exchange and interactions with FemDoms that may be undesirable or even harmful. They may be fine for someone else, but they aren't fine for you.

It is as essential to know when to say NO as it is to say YES. If you have difficulty saying NO in vanilla situations, you are going to want to teach yourself that skill before entering into kinky play.

Self-assured gentlemen who respect themselves and have the respect of others may not necessarily take those skills with them into kinky relationships. It may be because the need to connect with a FemDom is so strong, or it may be that the new rules of the kinky world are confusing, and the men have disabled their social firewalls because they feel that is the only way to find a FemDom. Either way, you have a responsibility to yourself and to the Lady of your future to reject people and activities that endorse lack of respect, isolation, or abuse.

Doorman vs. Doormat

One of the first things I heard coming into the BDSM world as a submissive/slave/bottom was that I wasn't a doormat. Neither are you. Now, if your kink is humiliation, you are going to be treated as doormat, because it's what makes your heart sing. Or, if you enjoy objectification and want a Lovely Lady to tread on you, and if you are really, really good, you get to be a doormat.

The rest of us, however, have very little interest in appearing to be or being treated as a doormat. As the gentleman of the hour, you may consider yourself a doorman. The difference is integral to your perception of self within a power exchange relationship. The doorman serves with intent and dignity. The doormat is used without consideration for its well-being. You are as valid as the FemDom. Without you, the power exchange cannot be complete.

No one has the right to use you without your consent. No one has the right to change the negotiation mid-scene. Even surprises are negotiated. At no point in any relationship, regardless of its brevity, are you to feel used and useless. If you do, it's your own fault. If you don't respect yourself and your judgment, why should she? You have legs; get up and walk away. If the questionable lady threatens you with rejection by the community in general or by every FemDom within 100 miles, laugh loudly and with feeling. Ladies of quality are awaiting your attentions. You do not need the user. If all else fails, tell her you are following my direction.

Consent vs. Abuse

Practically everyone I know has said this better, but I have an obligation to your welfare to state it again. If it feels wrong, it's wrong. If you wouldn't tolerate it before you met her, don't tolerate it now. If it felt great in your fantasies and hurts like hell in reality, say so. Use safe words. Those are code words to slow down or stop a scene. Red is for stop, and yellow is for slow down/check in with me, or whatever you negotiate before the scene. In my case, if I hear my given name, I stop. I know there's a problem. The reason we use safe words that are pre-negotiated is that the usual "Ow! Ow! Ow! Help, stop, no!" may be part of the scene and, thus, aren't going to change anything. Many Dominant Ladies enjoy hearing pitiful moans and abject pleas. Personally, I adore them.

At the first meeting with the Lady of your Dreams, remember to use a safe call. That's the person who knows where you are and who you are with and wouldn't mind calling the police on your behalf if he or she can't contact you at the specified time. Insist she use a safe call, too. If she won't, walk away quickly and with assurance.

You don't want to submit to a lady who does not put your safety and well-being first, before her wants. You want someone who accepts control, not takes it. Remember *Misery*, the movie in which an irate and irrational woman holds the writer of her favorite romance novel prisoner and breaks his ankle on purpose? That is certainly a scenario you want to avoid. Make the safe call. Prepare to live a long and happy life with the elusive Dominant Woman who would like all of her submissive gent's parts intact so she may use them as she pleases.

Once again, if you gave her permission, she can do it. If you didn't, she can't. There is plenty of time to negotiate a No-Limits contract. Early on in the relationship is not the time. In an online chat room is definitely not the time. No-Limits contracts are appropriate based on the mutual trust, honor and respect that develop over time. Although they appear to have no limits so that the FemDom can literally do anything she wants to the slave, the parties involved are so in sync with each other that they already know the limits of the relationship and do not choose to write them down.

Another pitfall to avoid in a kinky relationship is isolation, the restriction of social contacts as a stipulation of continuing the relationship. Isolation by your Dominant is an early red flag that something is systemically wrong. Don't jump right into the relationship before checking her out within her social circle. What? She doesn't have a social circle? That's another problem. Slow down, there, sweet boy. Join a submissives' group in your area. Ask for references. Play in public and attend public events.

Find a support group, even if it's only one kinky friend. Maintain contact with others who understand you and accept you, even if they don't share your kink. You can guess my reaction to that Supreme Goddess of the Eternal Pleasure who wants you to e-mail only her and communicate with no one else… that's right. Run. Flee. Your Mistress of the Future will appreciate your solid judgment.

Everyone I know has made goofy mistakes. I actually wanted to be submissive so badly that I renegotiated a scene in the middle of it and let a Dom handcuff me during a sensual scene that turned into Disciplinary Play. Thank heavens he was an experienced and caring Dom, and I had a wonderful time, albeit only once. Please don't make mistakes that cause you pain years into the future. There will always be another chance. Even if she feels right, she may not be.

It amazes me the reasons people give for rationalizing why a potentially harmful action could be supported or even desirable. Do you recognize these in yourself:

- "This will be my only chance."
- "No one else will ever want me."
- "If I contact my friends, she'll leave me, and I'll be alone."
- "I'm too old (poor, fat, stupid, pick your own adjective)."

Negative self-talk is more common than positive self-talk, and I'm afraid we listen to the voices in our heads as truth. If you are having trouble maintaining emotional distance and objective observation, pretend that whatever is happening to you is really happening to Fred. We both know that you are Fred, but it helps to write about someone we don't care quite so much about. Write Fred's experiences as a feature article in a newspaper. If you think Fred is making mistakes, look in the mirror and come up with a better plan. There are dozens of books on this very topic at your local used bookstore. I pick up one every couple of months or so and always learn something about myself. Invest in yourself and buy one.

I don't know your name, Dear Reader, but I worry about you. I want you to be happy and fulfilled, sitting at a Lady's feet, waiting to obey, but I question your judgment. Alas.

Pitfalls:
- Lack of respect
- Abuse
- Isolation
- Negative self-talk

Conclusion

In this chapter, you have separated power play from kinky play, a distinction that is vital in your quest to find wonderful play partners who may lead you to meeting more Dominant Ladies. You can identify seven areas of power play and select which ones you would like to match with your preferences in kinky play. You have analyzed some of the pitfalls of playing with power and are now ready to attack the inflexible and negative attitudes that may keep you from succeeding in your campaign to capture a Mistress.

Chapter Three
Leveling the Playing Field and Dispelling the Myths

The better you understand yourself and your kinky wants and needs, the better able you are to identify what you need in a kinky partner. You now have a list of kinky activities, as well as a concept of what kinds of power exchanges you desire. You have developed a filter to protect yourself from people who may harm you, either unintentionally or on purpose.

You may think it is time to find a partner. In truth, you may have thought it was time to find a partner about two chapters ago. However, in order to benefit from the gains you have made in the earlier chapters, it is essential to construct a new attitude about Dominant and submissive relationships, especially those concerning the FemDom. It is essential that your expectations, hopes and dreams can actually be fulfilled by a real, live Mistress and not a fabrication of your overactive imagination. More importantly, you should understand who you are and where you fit in.

Vanilla Relationships

If you are reading this with any interest at all, chances are you are kinky. You probably have vanilla, or non-kink, behaviors that make you socially acceptable in any situation. Admit it; you're kinky, and it isn't going to go away.

If you are kinky, then who are the vanilla people? The easiest way to define who is vanilla is to identify all of the people you know who wouldn't understand your inherent need to submit to a Dominant Female. At least, your negative self-talk convinces you they wouldn't understand. They are perceived as vanilla, and you are kinky.

I do not believe the world is separated into vanilla people and kinky people. I think it is more of a continuum, and it is perfectly normal to be anywhere on it. In addition, your kinky and vanilla needs may change as you grow throughout your life. This is your journey. No one has a right to determine for you which path to take, what to pack or how far to travel.

Hot Sex and the FemDom/Girlfriend

If you are looking for a girlfriend who likes hot, kinky sex, this book isn't for you. Go find a hot, kinky sex book. This book is for the person who knows deep within his heart that he must submit to a Dominant Lady of Quality. The sex is secondary to the primary need to submit.

From your earliest memories, you've been fantasizing about a Woman who takes control of both you and the situation. You give yourself freely and revel in her power. What's wrong with you? Absolutely nothing.

She's out there thinking the same thing. *What's wrong with me that I want to take charge and place a man at my feet? Why can't I find a good one?*

> ** Hot Tip: There's nothing wrong with either of you. You're perfect just the way you are.*

This isn't something your vanilla friends understand. It certainly isn't anything you want known at your place of business. Still, your desire to submit is there in every breath you take, in every word you speak. You are waiting for her. Read on, and begin a new path toward capturing, not a girlfriend, but a Mistress.

Here's more good news. She is not looking for a boyfriend. A boyfriend puts his own needs first, not hers. She wants you, a special someone who is happiest serving her. She is willing to wait for you, but it is your responsibility to prepare to serve and to make yourself known to her.

Maybe I'm Too Old

It helps if you have already made the mistakes that are worth making and now can embrace a new path in which you are seeking a lovely Lady of Dominance within a world that seems to hide her from your view. It helps if you understand women, if you know how to speak with them and what they desire. If you have read relationship books like John Gray's *Men are from Mars, Women are from Venus* and actually understand them, then you are ready for a relationship with a Dominant woman.

It's easier if you've had your children, and they are grown and have moved out of your domicile. You certainly may have a relationship with a FemDom, but it is more difficult if you have custody issues.

Some gentlemen assume if they are older, that they should have had some prior experience in the kinky lifestyle. Having a repertoire of kinky skills certainly is attractive to FemDoms. However, virgin experiences and fantasy fulfillment are just as valued.

All in all, older has its advantages.

Maybe I'm Too Young

On the other hand, you can be twenty-three with a two-year-old you have every other weekend and still make the perfect submissive for a Lady. It's all in the negotiation, and neither of you should have to give up anything. The world is your oyster.

The very attributes a younger man takes for granted in himself are treasured by a Dominant who is older and more experienced. Personally, I like playing the matron. Now, I don't want to ruin it for the FemDom, so I'll let her tell you why younger men are as delightful as older ones.

What if I'm a Wannabe?

You do not have my permission, now, or in the future, to refer to anyone as a wannabe. The same is true for you. No one is to call you a wannabe. If you don't have experience, and you are serious enough about your needs to read this book, you are a novice. Anyone who tells you differently is misinformed. Walk away.

In addition, I don't care how badly a Dominant or a submissive behaves, you are not to refer to that person as a wannabe. The person's poor behavior will speak for itself, and your input is unnecessary. It's also tacky. Tacky is not a quality a FemDom admires in a submissive male however accurate he may be at the time it is uttered.

What if I'm Not a True Submissive?

There is no such thing as a true submissive or a true (choose your own

41

noun), for that matter. To say so, means we are static and unchanging, not to mention boring.

The angst associated with the term "true submissive" may have come from Diane Vera's "Nine Levels of Submission" that appeared in the <u>Lesbian S/M Safety Manual</u> and shows up continually in chat rooms, on websites and in workshops. The work is over twenty years old (1984) and was probably not intended to promote insecurity and prejudice among the folks who associate themselves with the concepts of "bottom, submissive and slave."

In an attempt to sort people into nine different categories based on their perceived level of submission, Diane Vera labels them. The consequence of accepting a label or labeling ourselves means that we are now static, or stuck. Add to the mix that some of the labels are less than complimentary, and now it feeds into our negative self-talk. When we use words like "true", "real", "play" and "pseudo", they encourage value judgment over objectivity.

When I first entered the BDSM community, I was handed Diane Vera's "Nine Levels of Submission" to do a self-rating. I had a lot of difficulty with it, because it depended upon which person I was standing in front of, or kneeling, as the case may be, as to what my self-rating would be. Worse, it appeared that the higher the number, the better the person. At its very worst, the document was used to convince me I would never have what it took to be a true submissive slave.

Immediately, I topped over and became a FemDom and occasionally, a switch. However, I did it for the wrong reasons. I did it, because a mean-spirited Alpha slave believed she was doing the right thing by pointing out to me and anyone listening that I could never submit.

Currently, I am a FemDom almost every minute of every day, but that does not mean I'm dominant. It means I am exploring dominance, and at any point, I can explore submission. I get to decide this, not someone else, and especially not someone who doesn't have my best interests in mind.

It helps to have a little experience in the Leather world in which devoted slaves do not need to be submissive. The gift of obedience is all the greater when it is presented by a man who is normally dominant. Personally, I enjoy having a successful attorney naked at my feet..

In summary, you decide who you are, what you want and how you are going to get it. If checklists and rating scales make you feel good and validate your path, use them. If they make you feel superior to another person, put them away.

What If We Aren't Sexually Compatible?

Here is a misnomer if I have ever heard one. Sexual Compatibility. Everyone wants it. Not everyone gets it. My slave is 61 and is taking testosterone and Libidus™. I've had a mastectomy and am taking a drug to combat breast cancer that tells my body it has no need of any sexual stimulation. In other words, I have the libido of a floor lamp. C'est domage. Too bad. Ah, well, at least my body is not producing the cancer that is estrogen-fed. Still, it affects our relationship. I grant my slave the opportunities to have his sexual needs met when I am unable to participate due to the prescription drugs I take.

Negotiate. It will minimize your differences and maximize the elements in a relationship that are most important.

You may have a difference also. This will be your problem to solve. You will need to find the balance. Please consider out-of-the-box solutions. Both of you may need a mentor to explore new sexual practices. One of you may have more than one partner. One of you may have no partners. All is fair, as long as the needs of all the primary partners are met.

Can I Be a Slave if I Don't Have a Mistress?

Of course you can. You can create any world, convince others of its existence, and move in to live happily ever after. The male submissive who spends a lifetime preparing for his Lady of Dominance is ready. He needs only fine tuning to be perfectly trained. What could be better?

By taking positive action to prepare for her, you are paving the way for a seamless entrance into a kinky FemDom/male submissive relationship. Unfortunately, you may not know precisely what you need to do to prepare for her arrival.

* Hot tip: Prepare for the Mistress you wish to serve.

Create Her. If your vision is clear, she may choose to adapt her very predetermined preferences to meet yours, because she realizes her life will be enriched by your vision. Give her choices. As a male submissive, you have valid suggestions, just as valid as hers. Simply find a way to make them known with respect and humility. She shall treasure you, as she should.

However, in order to create her, you need to dispel the myths surrounding her.

Myths That Keep Us Unfulfilled

I feel one of the main reasons submissive males do not have a Lady in their lives is because they embrace myths that are detrimental to Dominant/submissive relationships or they attach themselves to ladies who believe in those myths.

The myth of **Soul Mate** is my favorite. Gentlemen contact me to ask if I am their one, true soul mate. They usually want to know this immediately, as if it is something you can plop in a shopping cart using the "Buy Now" option on eBay™. The myth of the soul mate involves there being a clandestine rendezvous between two people, who, when they meet, will instantly know it and move into a happily-ever-after without having to do any of the work it takes to get there, much less reside there, for any length of time. If one mate isn't working out, she must not be the Soul Mate; she was just an illusion, or worse, a siren. But, the one true Soul Mate is out there somewhere, and it's just a matter of time before she shows up.

Now, unfortunately, the Lady is taking the same passive approach to finding her Soul Mate. It's a relationship built on hope and inactivity, which is a recipe for failure.

Try turning it around. Try thinking that every woman you encounter is a soul mate. No, it probably won't work either, but at least it gives you practice attracting and serving Dominant Ladies. It gives the lady a chance to experience a dominant moment she may never have had if it hadn't been for you. Remember, I came into this kinky world on the submissive side. No one was more surprised than me when I topped over.

The second myth is the **Inequality in Love**. This is going to make me very unpopular. Some Mistresses believe it is imperative that if they are going to be successful Dominants, then they must not fall in love with their submissives. Now, I'm not sure you can control that sort of thing, but you can certainly control the perception of being in love.

I don't know that I am in love with my slave. I love him. I own him. The two are the same for me. Am I in love with him? No, probably not, but then, I don't like the idea of relinquishing that much control. Why would a normally rational person, either Dominant or submissive, try to engineer whether or not they are in love, especially if it is a decision made arbitrarily before they have met the partner? It's a recipe for failure.

If you get one of those Dominant Ladies who does not believe in falling in love with her special gentleman, accept it. She isn't in love with you. And for heaven's sake, stop asking her about it. Or, the opposite can be true, and you may need a degree of distance she does not. That is simply the way it is. Trying to change it creates discord in what was otherwise a pretty workable arrangement.

The third myth is the **More is Better** concept of derailing a perfectly good relationship. You see a couple at the local BDSM meeting and they have a third person with them. You want one or your Dominant wants one, but somebody wants something they don't have, and negative self-talk creeps in. *Why don't I have a third? Is there something wrong with me? That man is serving two Women, and I don't have anyone.*

Another example of **More is Better** occurs in the beginning of a relationship in which you have impressed a Lady, and she wants to spend more time with you. **More is Better** rears its ugly head, and you accept a collar. The myth is that having a collar is better than not having one. More is better.

Not necessarily. This is not a world of shortcuts. Your Lady and you have all the time in the world. I meet men who are in pursuit of a collar, not a Mistress. What they get is lots and lots of collars, but no long-term relationships, which is fine, if that's what they want. It usually isn't.

The other half of this myth is that now that we're in a long-term relationship, we should spend every waking minute together, move in with each other, or buy something together that won't be easily divided when one or the other of us needs more space or meets that ultra-monogamous third we call a home wrecker.

The myth of the **Long-term Relationship** is widespread. This is the one that says you can't be a real submissive until you are in a LTR (Long-term Relationship) with a Dominant Lady. In my opinion, you can be a submissive without at Dominant Lady in your life at all. You determine what you are, not your partner, and certainly not those Mean People whom you think can judge you. A one-night stand is perfect. A short-term relationship is perfect. It's all perfect, unless you decide you're going to be unhappy about it.

When I became divorced after twenty-five years of marriage, I grieved. If you need to grieve, do it. Grieving is perfect, too. Please accept responsibility for yourself, though. Grief, love, hate (or pick your own emotion) belongs to you, and I don't believe it is something another person can inflict on you. Once again, head to the used bookstore and find a self-help book on whatever emotion you are dealing with at the time.

Then there's the **I Can Stop Working Now** myth that renders a relationship impotent and unfulfilling. Sometimes it's the FemDom; sometimes it's the male. Eventually, it will be both. Yes, we should be content, but no, we never stop working to create a fascinating life for ourselves and our special ones.

The last myth is **It's All My Fault** followed by **It's All Her Fault**. She isn't going to like it any better than you are. If you don't make the other person wrong, and you don't make yourself wrong, there's a possibility you can resuscitate a relationship or at least terminate it on amiable terms. When a relationship is not working, others outside the two of you are not going to be able to put Humpty Dumpty together again, so there's no point in complaining about your particular situation to all the king's horses and all the king's men.

I know I have omitted myths that will simply have to wait for a reprint. It isn't that they aren't valid; it's that I missed them. Wait. That's another myth. **Mistress is Always Right**. Making her always right is as catastrophic to a relationship as making her wrong. She's human, and she'll screw up. Supporting her in every mistake she makes may not be as obedient as negotiating a way to indicate to her without the knowledge of others that she is heading down a path that may not be to her liking or intent.

My slave corrects me. I not only gave him permission to, I ordered it. One example is when we are going somewhere in two cars. I get lost. Worse, I don't seem to be able to remember where I've been and expect restaurants to show up in locations in which they aren't. Consequently, my slave has the responsibility to ensure, before I get into the vehicle, that we are both going to arrive at the same place at the same time. He is not questioning my ability; he is following orders. It's all in the perception.

Myths That Keep Us Unfulfilled:
- Soul Mate
- Inequality in Love
- More is Better
- Long-term Relationships are Best
- I Can Stop Working Now
- It's All My Fault (or Hers)
- Mistress is Always Right

Fulfilled:
- Every woman could be a Soul Mate
- Accept the love at whatever level she can give
- Stop searching for a Fantasy FemDom
- Envision the FemDom you wish to serve
- Ignore negative self-talk and judgments
- Prepare for the Mistress you wish to serve

Conclusion

In this chapter, you have taken a serious look at the attitudes and beliefs that may be keeping you from developing relationships with Dominant Ladies. However, now that you can "catch" yourself believing these myths and misperceptions, you have a better chance of "catching" a Mistress.

An M/s Studies Book

Chapter Four
Who is the FemDom, Really?

Who She is and Who She is Not

She gets to define who she is just like you get to define who you are. Both of you have different priorities, different standards and different goals in life. It is less important that your vision be identical to hers as it is that they mesh. Can you be a working pair, even if only for an evening?

Yes, you are going to be expected to modify some behaviors to suit her needs and wants. Yes, she will probably allow you a certain degree of freedom beyond what she may optimally desire. Such is the nature of compromise. I view compromise as the opportunity to create synergy, that alchemic experience that can not happen to either of you until you are together.

In my opinion, one of the misperceptions of power exchange is that it is a one-way street, making it preferable to land solidly on the Dominant side of equality. However, unless she has an incredible amount of time to micromanage you and desires to lavish her attention on you, she may want you to manage your own affairs right up to the point that she is affected by the outcomes of your decisions.

For example, if you are a smoker, and she is not, be prepared that she may expect you to quit. You will either accept quitting as part of the contract, or you will not. That is your choice, and no one is going to make you do anything to which you refuse to agree. Just don't expect her to compromise. It may be a deal breaker. The same is true for you.

In my case, my mother died of lung cancer directly linked to a long history of smoking. I have no intention of investing my resources, including love, in a long-term relationship with a smoker. On the one hand, the gentleman cannot expect me to change something so integral to my code of ethics. On the other hand, I cannot expect him to change a habit that gives him pleasure, and that he associates with a freedom that he will not sign over to me. We would be at an impasse.

Now, I would not throw out the baby with the bath water, nor do I, despite observations by my slave that occasionally I ascribe to that very technique. We have, however, moved the negotiations from Long-term Relationship to "something else." That something else is not determined until it is discussed openly. I do not create the male. I do not control the male. He does not create me. Nor does he control me.

This appears to be a misnomer, because it is all about power exchange. It isn't, however, about me taking it. It's more about the gift the FemDom receives when you offer it, and the solid understanding that nothing in life is permanent. That's what makes every interlude, every exchange, and every moment special.

In a power exchange, both parties have equal rights. They negotiate what their relationship is going to be and how those rights are going to be preserved. For example, the slave may not speak in formal protocol, but he has the obligation to speak in an emergency. He possesses the right; what the slave chooses to do with that right is what creates the basis of a Dominant/submissive relationship. A relationship in which the slave accepts speech restrictions is going to look vastly different than one with no speech restrictions.

Is She a Dominant or Just a Bitch?

One of the things inexperienced males tell me in confidence is that I am so different from the Dominant women they have met in the past. I challenge that assumption. They did not encounter Dominant women; they encountered bitches.

You need a bitch filter.

Because you want so much to serve, and because it is such an important element in your fulfillment as a vibrant, dynamic individual, you fall prey to being vulnerable to a bitch. If you see her for the bitch she is, you may feel guilty for your keen perceptions. Or worse, you may feel rejected.

For example, you see a lady descend the escalator. Her command presence seizes your attention. She barely notices you as others rush to make certain her papers are in order, her briefcase is available, and her path is cleared to move through the crowd efficiently. She barks an order at an intern who, startled and chagrined, scrambles to do her bidding.

Is she Dominant or just a bitch? At this point, it's difficult to tell. If you enjoy Humiliation Play, it's impossible to discern.

Let's approach this problem from a different angle. Let's assume she's a bitch until she proves otherwise. We've all known bitches. One may pop into your mind immediately. Frequently, she is an ex-wife whom you mistakenly labeled as a Dominant.

List the characteristics that help you define the woman as a bitch. Go ahead, write in the margins.   Later, you can look back on your notes and assess your growth. Or, you may present the notes to your Dominant Lady and let her use them as she chooses.

1. _____
2. _____
3. _____
4. _____
5. _____

Stop. I didn't trust you to write in the margins. Go back and do the exercise before you read my definition of a bitch. Your thoughts matter. Thank you.

I believe that the first characteristic that separates a Dominant from a bitch is self-control. A bitch is **not in control** of herself. She gets angry easily or behaves badly for inadequate reasons. She makes others uncomfortable without their consent. There is a lot or winning or losing in her speech patterns. You find yourself spending more time making certain she isn't irritated than in serving her.

The second characteristic is **low self-esteem**. Everyone has areas of vulnerability that result in a perception of inadequacy and are reinforced through negative self-talk. Do not choose a female who has a lower self-esteem than yours. She'll drag you down until yours is lower, or worse, she'll accuse you of topping from the bottom, a nasty term that means you'll never make it as a "true" submissive. Low self-esteem does not make her a bitch, but she'll be a bitch to live with, so it adds up to the same thing.

The next is **excess baggage**. I expect you to enter into a relationship without dragging into it every experience with every Dominant Woman in your address book. The same goes for the FemDom. It isn't your fault that her first husband stole her money, her second husband ran around on her, her third … you get the picture. It is, however, your responsibility to identify your excess baggage and get rid of it prior to entering into a long-term contract with her. If that requires therapy with a kink friendly therapist, get busy.

Whether you gain the attention of a Dominant Lady or a bitch, you are going to be judged by a **set of criteria**. This is the filter through which you must pass to earn the opportunity to enter into a Dominant/submissive relationship with her. One candidate for supremacy might screen out all men in certain age or weight groups. To another, it may be level of education or financial security that defines the filter. Each one is different, but if it is her set of criteria, and you can't get through her filter, you are very possibly not going to have a long-term relationship. You may, however, negotiate a play date or some other limited relationship.

She's not a bitch just because her filters don't allow you to pass. She's a bitch if she sets up one set of criteria and secretly judges by another. It doesn't matter to me if she's aware of it or not. This is the woman who tells you it's great if you have children and then objects to the time you spend with them. This is the female who professes she wants both of you to have an open relationship until you introduce your hot vanilla date to her. Then, she tries to make you feel inadequate, guilty, or at the very least, wrong. If she is dishonest in her dealings with submissive males, she falls solidly into the quadrant of bitch. If she's aware of what she's doing, she's a Queen Bitch.

Now, some of us are painfully aware that we are judging by two sets of criteria. I will forever and always use my ex-husband as one standard. We were married for twenty-five years; he may be out of the picture now, but he isn't going anywhere. Sometimes it's a good thing; sometimes it's not. The key, here, is that I know I do it. At no point have I made a decision concerning my relationship with a new male based on a previous experience with my ex.

Now, my slave may occasionally disagree, but I respect his opinion because, in cases that involve me, he is usually right. He knows I am one of those Dominant Ladies who will try very hard not to fall into the clutches of being just a bitch, and he doesn't mind helping me see the issue from another perspective.

Once you are in a relationship with her, is she a Dominant or a bitch? If she is constantly impeding the progress you are making on your path toward submission, or if she confuses leadership with a propensity for having her own way… you know what you have. **Poor judgment** is probably the most difficult characteristic to assess. No one practices poor judgment on purpose. It's like being a poor speller. No one does that on purpose either.

Don't serve a Lady who has worse judgment than yours. Look at her interpersonal relationships, look at her family, look at her job and her co-workers, look at her finances, and look at her living quarters. None of this is going to change because you show up. If you can't live with her exactly the way she is, you may be falling prey to your own poor judgment.

Oh, and if she has good judgment, she'll be assessing you, too.

Now, if you are an absolute ninny, a bitch is going to appear wise. If you are desperate, you can convince yourself you are in the presence of a Supreme Being. If you are lonely and so very tired of being alone, the bitch may appear Dominant. These are illusions, and you have a responsibility to sort them out ahead of time. Do not count on the lady in question to know whether or not she's a bitch. Judge her by her actions and not what she says, or you may end up with a bitch in Dominant's clothing.

> *Hot Tip: If you recognized any of these undesirable charac- teristics in yourself, you may wish to work on them. She isn't going to appreciate these qualities in you any more than you are in her.*

Occasionally, I still hear from a gentleman who believes from the bottom of his submissive heart that the perfect Dominant turned into a bitch. Overnight. No, she didn't. She was always a bitch. It's the gentleman's opinion that was changed overnight when he could no longer maintain the illusion of her supremacy.

Reread your list of what characterizes a bitch. My list is based on generic personal qualities I would avoid in anyone. They really have nothing to do with dominance. Is yours based on narrow personal experiences or fantasies? I encourage you to re-evaluate your criteria. If this is difficult, list the characteristics of a great friend and work backwards.

If you are still having trouble with the exercise, pretend you are marooned on a deserted island with the FemDom and imagine how you are going to get your basic needs met over the next few weeks. Pretend she is not as knowledgeable about survival. How will she react to your suggestions? How will you present those suggestions?

Now that you have solidly identified who you do not want in your life, you can list the Dominant's qualities that will create a situation in which you can serve without reservation. This should be a constitution, a document that does not change just because a really attractive FemDom shows up in fishnets and lacks one or more of the criteria essential for a strong relationship.

In addition, select criteria that you, yourself, strive to attain. This is not a wish list, nor is it a fantasy. It's a succinct list of values and characteristics that give you a filter by which to identify the next Dominant Lady in your life so that you may pursue her. Do not include criteria that you don't value, but are valued by friends, family, mentors, etc. It's difficult sometimes to tell how you are being influenced by others. The clearer the view, the better the list you can create.

These characteristics are mine. Your list may vary by an inch or a mile. Since it is your creation, it's right for you.

CHARACTERISTICS OF A DOMINANT

Characteristic	Evidence in behavior
In control of self	She will speak to others with respect and restraint, especially when there is conflict.
Good self-esteem	She will appear content and comfortable with herself, in both her speech and in her appearance. Others will want to be with her.
Light baggage	She will share adversities without making them personal or blaming others.
Filters you can pass through	She will not want to change me in ways I cannot change. She will not make negative comments about what I cannot change. She will not compare me to others.
Good judgment	Others will seek her out for counsel. She handles her life in a way that does not elicit a rescuing response.

If this chart does not meet your needs, create one of your own. Include what is most important to you and how you are going to know when she passes through your filter.

Will She Abuse Me?

Learn to tell the difference between the Lady using you in a way that is consensual and abusing you. What is use to one male submissive is abuse to the next. It is your responsibility to understand your needs and to short circuit abuse.

This means you have to apply your filtering checklist against what you have sitting in front of you in the way of a Dominant Woman. I choose to believe that if a gent tells me he's a submissive, he is. End of story. If his behavior and mine do not gel, that does not make him a poor quality submissive or a wannabe. It means our filters keep us from creating the world in which both of us choose to live. We still get to live there, just not with each other.

For each Dominant Lady, there is a different style, a different set of expectations, a different set of skills and interests, etc. The same is true for every male submissive. Promote tolerance and maintain distance. At no point should a submissive be labeled a failure for not meeting the Lady's expectations. The same is true for his judgment of her.

On the other hand, predators do not have the strong commitment to power exchange as a mutually fulfilling lifestyle. They assess; they take. Sometimes they leave a shell of a human being behind and choose to blame it on the victim. You can't avoid them entirely, but you can certainly develop a filter through which they cannot pass.

If you don't want to be a victim, don't be a victim. Predators have characteristics in common. **Isolation** is frequently the first. If the new love of your life wants you to terminate contact with your BDSM friends or submissive support group, run. Run away, not toward.

If you don't have BDSM friends, find some. They will be invaluable both as networking contacts and as a stabilizing factor in your kinky life. When you can't trust your own emotions and your bullshit filter has a hole in it, your friends may be able to help. Get yourself into a support group, even if it's online. The other submissives can't solve your problems, but they can listen, offer advice, and empathize. Some will have more experience than you do and may be able to act as mentors until you are in a more stable relationship.

If you aren't sure how to find a support group, do an Internet search on BDSM education organizations in your state. Contact one and ask to join the e-mail list for their submissive support group, which will usually have a catchy name that would not be identifiable on the e-mails that will be coming in.

* Hot Tip: Create an online kinky e-mail address that is separate from your vanilla ones. Don't make it vulgar.

It is important that you sort verbal abuse from correction. If the new Domme de Plume **threaten**s you with consequences that are damaging, physically, socially, or psychologically, walk away. This is the threat that she will ruin you in the BDSM community, or that you will never get a Domme after she tells everyone about you. If you wouldn't do it to a friend, she shouldn't be doing it to you.

Humiliation is the exception. I personally enjoy a level of humiliation, but only if I know the gentleman enjoys it, too. It's a form of negotiated play, however. I wouldn't just pull out the ball stretchers and TENS unit without prior negotiation. The same is true with humiliation. It's even more important, because the scars left are not physical. The Domme may not have a clue what her words or actions have created. They created baggage.

An abuser either **doesn't negotiate** or doesn't respect the outcome of those negotiations. View a reluctance to negotiate as a deal breaker. An abuser will use excuses to justify what she wants to do.

Excuses:
- If we talk about it too much, it will ruin the surprise (moment, shock value, experience, choose-your-own-noun, etc.)
- Real FemDoms don't negotiate; we lead.
- None of the true submissives ever want to negotiate. You want to be a true submissive, don't you?
- I just wanted to push your limits. You want to grow, don't you?
- Safe words are for (pick a derogatory subcategory of human)
- I don't want to talk about it. This is your problem. You don't (trust, love, obey, honor, worship, choose-your-own-verb, etc.) me.

Although these excuses seem transparent and absurd, when you are up to your eyeballs in lustful submission, your common sense may be the last thing you are interested in consulting.

** Hot Tip: If you want anything the abuser doesn't, she will make
you wrong for wanting it.*

Look in the closet on a daily basis. If you see more baggage today than
yesterday, this may not be the Domme for you.

Behaviors of an abuser
- Isolates you
- Threatens you
- Violates previous negotiations
- Blames you for self-preservation behavior

What's in it for Her?

Why would any woman in her right mind take on the responsibility for
the care and welfare of a submissive male? Many of us have children. If we
wanted another kid, we'd adopt. We already have all the pets we need. Some
of us are in helping professions. We're tired when we come home, and the
last thing we need is a parasitic, needy gentleman at our feet regardless of his
prowess in the bedroom. If that's the case, why do we do it?

Each FemDom will have her own reasons. You may never know why
she accepted you. You fulfill her wants and needs on enough levels that it is
desirable to keep you on a leash.

When my slave appears, I feel energized, not tired. He does not whine.
He is ever vigilant, looking for ways to make my life easier. He serves. He
waits. He takes direction and remembers how I like things done. He addresses me as Mistress, a title reserved only for my slaves.

My slave and I created our life together, not by kicking everyone else
out, but by living a life of power exchange while flying just below the radar of
all of the other people who are part of our world. It is seamless, and because
it cannot be consensual with vanilla people present, it is invisible. It's invisible
right up to the point that one of us slips, and we accidentally "out" ourselves,
or let others know we're kinky. It happens.

When I am with my slave, I feel honored that he chooses to spend time
with me. I believe he could have had any Dominant he would petition, but he

chose me. Every direction that he obeys, every expression he makes, every position he takes is a tribute to our relationship, and I treasure him. I am not able to fully articulate what he means to me and what I get out of the relationship with him. Sometimes, I choose not to over analyze.

Now, the only person who is going to know what she gets out of the relationship is the Domme of your Dreams. If she can't articulate it, help her. Ask questions and not the same ones.

This does not mean it is easy for her, nor should you pry. However, by understanding what she gains from the relationship, you are better able to serve, to submit. If she understands what she reaps, she will be happier sowing it with you and not someone from her fantasies.

One of the pitfalls of this type of analysis is that there are bound to be areas that the Domme needs that you cannot fulfill and vice versa. If she has a need and you cannot meet it, it is your responsibility to assist her in getting that need met. She will treasure you for understanding, and may very well be tolerant when you express a need that has a low-level priority for her.

In our case, I am a spanko. My first sexual thoughts were of spanking. I adore the power exchange, and I enjoy switching. My slave is a Leather slave who has a permanent slave of his own. He cannot, no matter how hard he has tried, become a spanko, which I believe to be a sexuality one is born with, not earned. Therefore, I go to spanko parties and leave him to his own devices. He's miserable if I take him along. He can't stand others touching me, much less throwing me over the couch and paddling the hell out of me. It's better to leave him home.

Because he is supportive, I find myself being more tolerant of our differences. My slave rarely has to sacrifice anything to be with me. Each gift is a gift. He loves multiple sex partners, and I grant him permission to have those relationships, as long as it does not adversely affect the one he's having with me. We fulfill one another's needs to the best of our abilities. In the areas in which we are not compatible, we encourage each other to enjoy the journey alone or with someone else.

Conculsion

For you, the relationship may be very different than the one shared by my slave and me. Who you are is just perfect, and the work you have done thus far is valuable. Your bullshit meter has been calibrated. Your Domme filter is coming along nicely. Now, it's time to figure out how to get along with a FemDom once you find her.

Chapter Five
Getting Along with the FemDom

What She Can Do for You and What She Can't or Won't

The better you are able to articulate your needs and the reasons for your submission, especially to her, the better able she can meet them. That doesn't mean she will meet them herself. You get her, when it's a match. When it isn't, you get to wait or you get what you negotiate.

The Dominant Female needs you as much as you need her. You may love her more. You may demonstrate that need more often, but it is there. If she doesn't need you, why are you hanging around?

She can give you the benefit of her strengths. If she is highly organized, do it her way. If she is a gifted conversationalist and you trust her to pass as your vanilla date, invite her to your office mixer. Every shared experience strengthens your relationship and tie to her.

You may want to show her off to friends, family, or the BDSM community. Nothing says this is going to be okay with her. She may not do this for you, especially if she needs to maintain a low profile or finds extroversion unfulfilling. My slave dearly loves to serve me in public, whether I request it or not. In a posh restaurant, he holds my door…good, I like this. He seats me at a table I like and facing a view I appreciate…good, I like this, too. I smile at him, and we share our special moment together. He places the cloth napkin across my lap with a reverence that is not lost on me. Then, for whatever reason, and I don't know what possesses him, he kneels at my feet and kisses my water glass before presenting it.

Heads turn. Mouths open. I sigh. He's done it again. And, he's fast, so if I don't want the nonplussed stares from perfect strangers, I need to give the order that he is to remain seated before the water glass arrives. He does not disobey, but on the other hand, he doesn't miss an opportunity for Goddess Worship. In my defense, I treat it as an everyday occurrence, which it is, and let the onlookers think whatever it is they think. Most appear to think they didn't see what we know they just saw.

Macromanager vs. Micromanager

Macromanaging is when the FemDom gives a direction or instruction, and she is more concerned with the outcome, not necessarily how it gets done or by whom. One Dominant friend of mine is constantly "outwitted" by his slave who follows the direction, but finds other, more effective ways of achieving it. Because the slave is a professional, he does not have the time to mow the lawn. He hires it done and supervises the service. His Owner appreciates that the lawn is mowed and doesn't care how it was accomplished, despite his pretense of grumbling about it. This is macromanaging.

I'm a macromanager. I don't care what steps it takes to create pesto. I like pesto. I want pesto. I don't care who makes it, how much it costs or who spent hours in the kitchen doing whatever it is that chefs do to create it. I just want some on Tuesday night.

My slave is a micromanager. He has his own slave. He has to own a slave, because the process for achieving the task is as important as the outcome, if not more so. As an example, he has written Protocols: Handbook for the female slave by Robert J. Rubel, PhD, which began as their protocol manual for creating their daily lives together.

As long as he'll leave me alone and won't try to micromanage me, the relationship works. My slave is a master at managing time, resources, and the process leading to the product. He can tell you exactly how many minutes it takes to do practically anything, assuming you are willing to follow his directions explicitly. His slave chooses to memorize extensive checklists, protocols and rituals. I choose not to, although by the very nature of living together, a certain amount of protocol seems to be rubbing off on me. We live together, but respect each others' differences. And we all eat pesto.

If you need macromanaging, say so. If you need micromanaging, say so. If you need a combination, figure out what it is and articulate it before problems occur. She is not a mind reader. She may know precisely what she wants, but may not have pondered through all of the steps to get there. She may find the steps are as important, if not more important, than the outcome. If this is so, you need to know about it.

Make a list of all of the responsibilities you expect to have in serving a Lady. This can be a soup-to-nuts list beginning with keeping the car filled with gas to elaborate foot massage/pedicures and anything in between. If it isn't going to bother you to follow her directions on completing the task, mark it with a yellow highlighter for "Micromanagement Tolerant". If you really feel you need to complete the task but she does not need to be consulted until it is time for her approval at completion, or if you think you have a better method and would just as soon be left alone to accomplish it, mark it with a green highlighter for "Macromanagement Preferred".

If there is more yellow than green, you are seeking a FemDom who enjoys supervising you and may want to check up on your progress, rewarding you accordingly. If you have more green than yellow on your checklist, you are seeking a FemDom who wants to know that the project is complete, when it was completed, how much time or resources it took, but probably won't do much with the information, as long as you use your time effectively and follow her directions to her specifications. She will reward you at completion of the task. If you have about the same amount of green and yellow on your check-list, you may be flexible in your service, giving you the opportunity to please more FemDoms.

It is worth it for you to know which management style you prefer. That does not mean you have to adhere to it. You can certainly experiment with your tolerance and appreciation of different styles as you create relationships with those Dominant Ladies.

MICROMANAGING OR MACROMANAGING

Responsibility	Micromanagement Tolerant	Macromanagement Preferred
Grocery shopping		
Chauffeur service		
Phone protocols		
Breakfast preparation		
Other		

Do not expect a FemDom to know what management style she prefers. She knows how she likes things done and which tasks she wants you to do. Although you may not ask her if she is a micromanager or a macromanager, you can certainly ask questions and gauge her responses accordingly.

For example, view the task below and infer the reason for asking for clarification:

- Task: She assigns that the oil in her car is to be changed by next Tuesday at 6:00 p.m.
- Clarification: "Yes, Ma'am, I will have the oil changed by next Tuesday at 6:00 p.m. Are there any other directions specific to how I accomplish this, or would you like me to handle it and report the details to you Tuesday evening?"

If she gives a detailed list of where to take the car for service, which brand of oil and that the car is always washed after service, follow the directions and record in your journal that she likes to micromanage oil changes. If she doesn't give you any detailed directions, she macromanages oil changes.

The problem occurs when Lovely Lady perceives herself to be a macromanager, but really wants to micromanage the task. She may not be aware that she is doing it, but when you change the oil your way, she may be surprised you did the task yourself rather than going to the mechanic on the corner who has always serviced her vehicles. You are not a mind reader. She may not know her management style for all tasks. Neither person is to blame for the lack of communication. Discuss it, record the results and make certain you follow directions to her satisfaction next time, regardless of whether or not the task needs micromanaging.

One difficulty you may encounter is the negative self-talk that surrounds micromanaging. You may think that the Lady does not trust you to accomplish a task correctly. You may feel inadequate when she looks over your shoulder or corrects a minute difference in the way you are completing a task. Neither may be true. She doesn't need to direct you; she wants to. Therefore, please her by following her directions and reporting your success.

Slaves of micromanagers have far more opportunities to practice obedience and perfect their service. Slaves of macromanagers have more opportunities to demonstrate ingenuity, time management skills, consumer skills, etc. Be flexible in that some tasks will be micromanaged and some will be macromanaged.

Ride the Horse in the Direction it's Going

If the horse is heading toward the stream for water, and you are on top of the horse, you have a choice. You can work really, really hard to keep the horse from drinking, or you can go to the stream with the horse and make it a perfect experience.

Who is in control? Who has the reins? The difficulty is discerning when you have a situation in which you are making the decisions and when you have one in which your Lady is making the decisions. To compound the problem, there are times when you or she wants to have control and neither of you are going to succeed, as in the case of chronic illness.

It helps if both of you have a solid comprehension of your needs and wants, and don't confuse them.

If it isn't worth fighting over, don't. If you know that she can't have an orgasm without foot play, play with her feet. If she is determined to run for office in your local BDSM organization, assist her. Whether she wins or not, she'll remember your valuable assistance. In other words, if she wants to get a drink from the stream, and it doesn't violate your needs or ethics, go with her and make it a perfect experience.

She may have needs that do not meet your wants. If she needs multiple slaves or submissive gentlemen, you are either going to have to accept them or leave. Polyamory is a state of being, not a practice she is going to want to sacrifice to be with you. You can, however, jockey for position among the gents. You can be top dog, as long as you can be both the Dominant to the men and the submissive to your Lady. Or, when she wants multiple men, she may excuse you to do those activities she does not find fulfilling, but knows you do.

Ride the horse in the direction it's going. As an analogy, if we wanted to ride horses, my slave would pick English dressage; I'd be a die-hard barrel racer. Most of us spend too much time trying to change or improve the partner. My partner, who is also my slave, has a fetish for protocol. He adores dressing in military garb for semi-formal dinners and serving multiple courses complete with linen service. The plates are one inch from the table's edge. I've never seen so much silverware. It goes on and on. See his book. Micromanager.

I, however, like dining nude on the patio on paper plates overlooking the sunset and eating with my fingers. Is this going to work? Of course, it is. Once we've defined our differences and similarities, it's a matter of negotiating what we're willing to do to make ourselves and the other person content.

Every morning at precisely ten o'clock, he prepares breakfast and serves me on the patio in whatever state of disarray I choose to present for the occasion. Every evening, I arrive at table dressed in formal military garb, or Chinese silks, or whatever he selects for a delightfully elaborate semi-formal dinner. He serves me. His slave serves us both. I have learned to appreciate fine dining, fine food and a love of protocol that I hadn't thought possible.

I'm not sure he's learned anything, but he doesn't fuss anymore when I help set the breakfast table by depositing everything in the center of it. Still, he gets to present morning coffee to me on his knees.

We are accomplished equestrians. Both ride the horse in the direction it's going. Since it is our world that we have created, we are not concerned that others might find it lacking or not a "true" Mistress/slave relationship or whatever it is they choose to think. We've created our own happiness, and it doesn't get any better than this.

Ride the horse in the direction it's going. Create your world, and if there are parts of it you cannot control, you can control your reaction to it. You can find ways to make going to the stream absolutely perfect.

Assess Needs and Wants with an Eye To Compromise

They can't all be needs no matter how badly you want them to be. Daily, each of us assesses needs and wants and how resources can be used to manage those selections. The same applies to preparing to serve a Lady of Dominance. In finding that special Someone, are you listing your needs or are you fantasizing about an unattainable number of wants?

What do you need in a relationship with a Dominant woman? Try listing all of the possibilities and specific desires you have and then sort them into Needs and Wants. You may want a lady with a Mae West figure, but do you need it? On the other hand, if that's part of your fetish, it falls very solidly into the Need category and you shouldn't settle for less. Your list is just as valid as anyone's.

What is less? Less is when you give up a Need you have either because you decide it is unattainable or the One whom you wish to serve doesn't possess it. I do not recommend sacrifice. I recommend negotiation. If it's a Need, it stays a Need. Wants, on the other hand, may change. If your Needs list is longer than your Wants list, you may either be too picky or very focused and know exactly what you must have to form a special relationship. It's hard to tell.

> *Hot Tip: Don't create a Needs and Wants list with a specific FemDom in mind. It will skew the results.*

Take another look at the Needs list. Try to imagine your life without one of them. If it is tolerable, switch it to the Wants side of the sheet. If you can't imagine life without this Need, write it in capital letters and don't compromise.

What you are doing is creating a Domme Filter. Ladies with potential will either make it through the filter to your next level, or they will not, and you will not have wasted time. Dommes who do not make it through the filter can be friends, acquaintances or one-night stands. Please don't make them enemies.

Have you ever met a FemDom or a submissive male who seems to go through endless possible partners? The Domme-a-Day works out for a brief period of time and then the filters come into play and either one or the other ter- minates the relationship. There is absolutely nothing wrong with this approach, as long as neither you nor she is wrong when it doesn't work out. It's rather like wanting a black shirt and snatching something black off the sale rack without looking at size, price or style. Chances are it won't be in your closet very long if it isn't right for you.

The Domme-a-Day approach to capturing your personal Lady does have its benefits. You can learn how to serve and please several ladies, all of whom are possible references. If you know the FemDom is not going to make it through the Long-term Relationship filter, say so up front. You may have accidentally made it through hers. During your brief time together, you can profit from her experience, as well as travel a bit further on your submissive journey. Both of you should be satisfying your wants, if not your needs.

For example, She loves fine wine and cheese. You're sort of a Longhorn Colby guy who buys his wine in a box. Be honest with her and offer service in trade for skills in the appreciation of wine and cheese. Learn from her. Treasure her. Thank her. You may always be a wine-in-a-box kind of guy, but you will know when to offer your newfound knowledge as a gift of submission to the next Lady, whether she falls into the Domme-a-Day category or one closer to your heart.

As the Dominant in a relationship, I am not interested in recreating the wheel. Take peanut butter sandwiches. I like them made one way, and I'm willing to train a gent to do it precisely to my liking, especially if he has a for- mal fetish and finds peanut butter unappetizing… yes, love, I'm a sadist. The inverse of this is also true. I am not interested in teaching a gentleman basic table manners he could have acquired from any etiquette book found in a used book store. Each Lady may be different, but the more skills you have, the more time you have open to learn the intimate details of meeting her Wants and Needs.

What If our Kinks Don't Match?

You know what you have been fantasizing about forever. She has fantasies, too. Sometimes those fantasies turn into kinky activities with wonderful partners. Other times, they are best left to the realm of fantasy. It usually takes a few mistakes before we remove the fantasy from our activity list or compromise and create the Next Best Thing.

The easiest way to match kinks with a possible partner is to pair activities. There are numerous checklists on the Internet. Many list the degree to which you would be willing to perform an act. The danger is that what turns you off might turn her on and vice versa. In addition, what you think turns you off could, in time, be a cherished activity you crave.

Beware the pitfalls of checklists. When I entered the BDSM community, I entered as a submissive female who most desired to be a Gorean slave, a captured sex slave taken from the steamy pages of John Norman's fantasy novels. One of my first "assignments" was to fill out a BDSM checklist of activities. Dutifully, I researched all of the activities I had never heard of and spent hours and hours filling out the checklist. He was doing the same, as was his Alpha slave, or First girl.

Within the first few minutes of the interview, the Dominant male asked me my hard limits, called "Hard Nos." I replied that I didn't know what they were, but I would try not to have any. He immediately told me to undress, step into the bathtub where he intended to relieve himself onto my shoulders, which is called a golden shower. I was thrilled and hopped up to obey. That was the last thing he expected me to do. Because it was a hard limit of his, he assumed it would be one for me also. Such was not the case. We both learned something about interviews and checklists. We are friends to this day, and I cherish all that I learned from him.

Shortly after, we discovered that being a Gorean slave wasn't my calling. With the help of the local BDSM community, I topped over and now consider myself a switch in FemDom mode almost all of the time. Yes, I am willing to serve a special Someone, but the need is not so strong that I enter into the relationship lightly or frequently.

I don't use checklists now, in part, because my kinks are more service oriented and don't show up specifically on most checklists. I do, however, ask gentlemen to evaluate desire or fulfillment from an activity by rating it from one to ten. These are verbal negotiations, and I do not write down anything until we are closer to play. Because I am a psychological Domme, the negotiations are as much a part of play as are the activities, if not more so.

Communication is the key to negotiating and getting the needs of both parties met. Not everything has to be communicated in the first few hours of the relationship. So many times, good candidates for submission mess it up by stating very clearly what they can do for the Lady of their Dreams, and then telling them verbatim what the Mistress should do to please them. The Mistress is going to please him when the man has performed and earned a reward for his service. Maybe. She isn't going to please him because he can articulate his pleasures. She assumes he knows what they are and can service himself until the time comes that he earns the privilege of her attention. Or, she may not allow him to service himself at all because orgasm denial is one of her kinks.

Now, just because the male sub is a swinging stud who beds women nightly and the Lady of his Dreams is into orgasm denial, doesn't mean they can't have a wonderful relationship. In the contract they can list the parameters and the limitations of their partnership.

For example, my slave is a swinger. My interest is less than minimal in anything that doesn't have a strong psychological component to it, and in my limited and somewhat prejudiced opinion, partner-swapping does not qualify. Does he have to give it up because I won't participate? No, but he does need to ask to be released to go to a swinging party, because he knows I will not be attending.

On the other side of it, I am a life long spanko, and I can't wait until the next party. My slave has endured two parties. During the first ten minutes of the second party, a consummate spanker, and one of my favorite partners, threw me over a convenient piece of furniture, and my slave went silently bat shit crazy which affected his blood pressure and his ability to speak. Needless to say, we have resigned ourselves to the common sense approach that we are not going to be able to fulfill all aspects of each other's needs at all times.

*   Hot tip: We're human. Sequitur: So are you.*

Too many gentlemen enter into a relationship with a Lady thinking that if he serves her beverages, rubs her feet and addresses her as Grand Duchess of the Multiple Orgasms, she will attend to him in the exact manner of his fantasies. No, she doesn't have to dress you in pantyhose and send you into the department store to buy a six-gartered girdle. She may do that as a reward for service, but she doesn't have to. This is a safe, sane and consensual world we live in.

On the other hand, you don't have to be her toilet slave, pain slut or cuckhold, unless you find that erotic. The key is to find the match and to earn the privileges of having your needs met with the partner of your dreams.

Separate reality from fantasy. Later, we will explore how reality and fantasy can occur at the same time, but for right now, tease them apart.

FANTASY AND REALITY

Fantasy	Need	Reality
Paraded nude in the grocery store	Humiliation	Nude on the balcony of the apartment with the fear of exposure and a bath towel
Strapped until you're bleeding for sassing	Domestic discipline, punishment/forgiveness	Spanked, corner time, scolded, forgiven
Forced to service a captor all night long	Forced sex, surrender	Faux abduction, service that coincides with dosage of Viagra™

As long as your needs are getting met, you can keep your fantasy and function well within the safe, sane and consensual constraints of reality.

Setting Yourself Up for Failure

Talk to anyone about it. The chance of a 24/7 D/s long-term relationship succeeding is slim. I'm sure there is research out there, but common observation can arrive at the same conclusion with a lot less work.

You know it's 24/7 if the people primarily involved are within physical touch of each other for at least as many hours in a day as the typical married couple. You know it's D/s if there is a Dominant/submissive power exchange in which one partner voluntarily offers to submit to the other partner, and the other partner accepts. Each relationship is different; you do what works for you and your Lady. Unfortunately, many kinky people decide that a 24/7 D/s relationship is the only one worth having, and then they mess it up.

I believe one thing a submissive male does to sabotage a relationship is to set himself up for failure. This doesn't make any sense at all, but we're human, and everyone does it until we can identify the process and change it.

To clarify, in the vanilla world, your friend tries to quit smoking cold turkey, in one instant. However, he doesn't change any of the habits that accompany smoking. He isn't taking any medication, nor has he asked his friends for help. Therefore, he still drives the same route to work and hasn't emptied the ashtray or removed that half pack of cigarettes that is still in the glove compartment. After one week, he can't figure out why he's smoking again.

Unfortunately, many of us use the same degree of care and planning in our vanilla relationships, and we're surprised when the divorce papers arrive.

There is no excuse for this in the kink community. We are a community grounded in communication and contracts. Therefore, we need to know and to agree with what goes in them, and just as importantly, what is left out of them.

If you approach a Dominant Lady and wish her to consider your petition, which is the basic level contract, what are you going to put in it? I get petitions submitted online, and although I respect the gentlemen's offers, I can't consider them seriously. Why? Because, they are creating a situation in which they cannot succeed.

For example, in his fantasy, a submissive male wants desperately to be enslaved by the wicked goddess who despises him for his weaknesses and rejoices in humiliating him about the size of his penis, which is permanently locked in a cock cage that leaves a conspicuous bulge through his clothing.

Now, this is great fun in the bedroom and can even be carried into public restaurants, if we're careful and discreet. It cannot, however, survive at the Thanksgiving table with Aunt Gertrude. It has less of a chance of survival if the gentleman is in a car accident and breaks his hip. Or, there's the problem of a recurring urinary tract infection he forgets to tell her about. Or, he's losing sleep, because he sleeps on his stomach, and it's not as comfortable with his cock locked in that over-sized cock cage. She understands her foolishness when he rolls over and train-whistle snoring emanates from his side of the bed.

How could this couple have set themselves up for success? It isn't that difficult, but it has to do with flexibility. Many Dominants and submissives are enslaved, not by the contract, but by their very limited view of what a D/s rela-tionship is supposed to look like.

For example, the male submissive finally gets an interview with a pro-spective Mistress, and he doesn't want to offend her or appear to be "topping from the bottom", which is a term used when the Dominant perceives that the submissive is telling her what to do when the information is not wanted. To avoid topping from the bottom by making excessive demands, the submissive male doesn't make any requests, and the prospective Mistress is expected to create the entire relationship. Or worse, she recreates what didn't work last time, hoping this guy will be a better slave.

By being flexible, you can compartmentalize your lives together into sec-tions based on time, setting or function. Every day after work, she may expect you naked and kneeling in the foyer when you hear the garage door close. If she's bringing home a vanilla friend, she may expect you to be dressed in a suit, to open the door for her and to serve cocktails on the balcony, but she's called ahead, so you are fully dressed and have checked to be certain that the liquor cabinet is stocked. That works.

Today, though, she's wearing that special strap-on and has rewarded you with an evening of hot sex and cock and ball torture. She's been teasing you about it all week, and finally you negotiate the way the evening will go. That works.

However, if Aunt Gertrude arrives unexpectedly, you need an emergency plan so that Mistress's strap-on and your gag don't become a legend at the church social every Wednesday night for years to come.

Flexibility means planning what to do when things go poorly, as well as planning when things go well. It means that both of you know what success feels like so you may create it. It's no fun trying to resurrect one perfect night that happened two years ago. Manufacture new predicaments and exciting lives together. Just remember to detail escape plans, if someone pulls the fire alarm in your apartment building at three o'clock in the morning.

Now this all sounds very funny, and someday I will write a book about the hilarious things that have happened to kinky couples. The "setting yourself up for failure" syndrome also happens in relationships. The submissive male may expect an order when the Dominant Lady thinks he should have the sense to realize when the furnace filter needs to be changed. Relationships have cratered on less.

Flexibility does not mean giving up any Dominance or submission. It means you both can compartmentalize your lives to get your needs met.

Priorities create another problem that can incinerate a budding D/s relationship. If you know you have an ailing mother, there needs to be a contingency in the contract. If the Lady of your Dreams can't handle that, guess what? You only have one mother. Get a better Mistress.

Your priorities are as set as hers. She knows what hers are, and you know what yours are. Write them down and discuss them. After the "givens" are determined, such as family, health, religious practices, create priorities that are relevant only to your life together, your compartmentalized fantasy world in which reality co-exists, and most of the time, life is wonderful.

Flexibility enters into it when you realize one of your priorities may not be one you have to handle. Perhaps you could hire someone else to care for that elderly parent on occasion. Yes, your dog can indeed go to the kennel while you are taking that cruise to Tahiti. No, the dog won't like it, but frankly, you'd better place more importance on your Mistress than on your dog. Relationships have cratered on less.

It's an open discussion void of D/s role play, and I strongly recommend you and the Lady of your Dreams figure out a way to have them, and with frequency. If you want her to consider being flexible about one of her priorities, figure out how to say it without making her feel as if she is wrong. Or worse, stupid.

Turn-ons and Turn-Offs

When pursuing a Lady, it helps if you don't do something stupid. There is a laundry list of stupid things men can do in the name of submission. Avoid the ones listed below, and at least whatever you do will be original.

Most of us respond to a bit of formality that appears to others as southern hospitality. Learn to seat a Lady. Know how to open a door and practice it at every opportunity. This is trickier than it looks and requires noting the location of the door hinges, especially if more than one door is involved. Manage elevator doors and push the buttons. Practice introductions and ordering from menus. This is advertising. Dominant ladies notice manners immediately, and naturally gravitate toward males who may be submissive.

Keep a journal or tracking sheet for your service behavior. You are practicing submission until a Dominant Lady recognizes what you are and wants you in her life. Consider using a special, locked online calendar on your computer to track your progress. This record, or a summary of it, can be submitted to a prospective FemDom as part of your petition, should she request it.

You may prefer a chart similar to the one below. Each day, tally or write anecdotal comments that describe the type of service you offered to a Lady and how many times you performed it. It doesn't matter whether or not she accepted the service, unless you see a pattern of rejection. Keep track of data and notice trends. You may wish to have a chart for weekends, one for weekdays and one for evenings. Personalize this chart to create your own.

SERVICE PRACTICE

Service	Date	Person	Location	Comments
Opened door-car				
Opened door-building				
Let a lady go first				
Pushed elevator buttons for a lady and let her go first				
Served a lady food or drink				
Used Ma'am or similar words				

Deferred to a Lady's judgment when you knew it was correct				
Corrected a lady in a respectful and sub-missive manner				
Offered assistance to a lady in need (pen, reach something, etc.)				
Thanked a lady for assistance or service				
Thanked a lady for allowing you to assist or serve				
Assisted or served a lady without her request				
Choose your own.				

If you do not immediately see the benefit of keeping a chart of your submissive behavior, practice using it for one week and journal what you have learned. I see far too many gentlemen who want to be submissive males who don't advertise their skills through public service and who don't perform services until they've snagged a Mistress. I view the former as poor business sense and the latter as procrastination at best, and delusion at worst.

In addition to tracking your success in service, keep a personalized list of mistakes you have made. These should be good stories for later, after you have captured a Mistress. Below is a brief list of DON'Ts when meeting a prospective Mistress.

1. Don't call her "Honey." She'll never be your girlfriend, but she might be your Owner.
2. Don't call her "Mistress." She'll give herself a special name for you to use when she feels the time is right.
3. Don't assume you know what she wants you to call her. The default is "Ma'am", but it is appropriate to ask.
4. Don't assume you have permission to address her, touch her, or serve her as others do. You don't know the relationships she has with them.
5. Don't usurp the responsibilities of the slave she's been training by holding the door or any other polite gesture. You wouldn't interrupt a working dog, would you? Her slave-in-training should receive the same respect.
6. Don't assume she has any interest in downcast eyes or silence or kneeling. She knows what she wants, and she'll tell you when the time is right.
7. Don't talk too much or tell more about yourself than she wants to hear or is socially appropriate. In other words, between "Hello" and "How are you?" she doesn't want to know your deepest fantasies and how good you are in bed.
8. Do not assume you know what she thinks is erotic or kinky.
9. Don't send her an elaborate e-mail until she gives you permission. It is acceptable to request a third party introduction via e-mail, or if you don't have a mutual acquaintance, to submit a very brief request for an e-mail

exchange, offering references, if you have them. Do not send a pic of your privates or any other part of you, unless she requests it. A penis on a male is considered the default.

10. Don't assume she's Leather, or Gorean, or (pick your kinky subculture). She'll tell you when the time is right, if there are not enough nonverbal cues to figure it out on your own.

11. Just because she indulges in a fetish with a special one does not mean she wants to take on a new partner in the same activity. She may have needs the gentleman at her feet cannot fulfill. Perhaps that will be your job.

12. Do not malign your previous Mistress, even if she is a malevolent sow, and you're glad you divorced her.

13. Don't say anything to her that you can't back up. For example, if the yacht belongs to your boss, it belongs to your boss. It is considered lying if you leave her with the impression that it's yours.

Master this list and you will be ahead of your peers in the pursuit of Mistress.

Love is a One-Way Street

She may never love you or be in love with you. Get over it. Love is a state of mind that is entirely in the control of the person experiencing it. I give you permission to love her and to be in love with her. I also give her permission to NOT love you and to NOT be in love with you.

In the Leather world, there is a controversy as to whether or not the Master should be in love with the slave. Often, the slave is in love with the Master. Some say once a Master is in love with the slave, the slave has too much control and will dominate the relationship. Others state that if they invest that much time and energy in a relationship, love is the least they expect out of it.

It is my opinion that slaves choose their Mistresses, not the other way around. That is more of a Leather approach, but it works for me.

You have to assess your own needs and create what works for you. You have to know if it is okay if you love her, but she doesn't love you. If you need mutual love, you will need to find a special Dominant Lady who feels the same way.

On the other hand, it is possible through sheer willpower, to convince a Lady who has no intention of loving you, that indeed she does. It happens. It happened to me. No, I certainly didn't want it. I even rebelled against it. Over five years I have learned to love him, but not be in love with him. He's okay with that, mostly because he has learned to ride the horse in the direction it's going.

Speaking of love, Gary Chapman defined it as well as any. *The Five Love Languages: How to Express Heartfelt Commitment to Your Mate* is a handbook (ISBN 1-881273-10-5) published in 2004 that gives you an understanding of why a loving relationship didn't work out and how to recognize and appreciate acts of love even if they aren't something you would normally associate with the concept of love. It is important that you know how you want love expressed to you. I did not say "need." I said "want." It is equally as important that your FemDom knows her language of love. Obviously, both of you need to share that information with each other, preferably in the form of a contract.

There are five languages of love, according to Chapman:

1. Words of Affirmation: You may never say, "I adore you, Mistress." She may need to hear it daily.
2. Quality Time: You may require a special time alone together to feel totally loved in your new relationship. She may have a full-time job, young children to care for and commitments in the evenings. She wants you to settle for a phone call three times a week.
3. Receiving Gifts: If either one of you needs gifts to feel loved, the other of you had better figure it out and come forth. Gifts do not need to be expensive. A sticky note saying something special attached to her monitor or yours may suffice.
4. Acts of Service: You may not be allowed to say, "I love you," but your service will stand as a declaration of that very love.
5. Physical Touch: You may not be allowed to touch your Lady. You may have an incredibly strong need to be touched by her.

In the Dominant/submissive relationship, it is important that both parties feel accepted for the language of love they bring to the relationship, as well as accept the other party's language of love as genuine. Although this would not be part of the initial petition to serve a FemDom, it is excellent conversation upon which to build a contract.

The danger arises when one party dismisses the acts of love of the other party. It isn't a deliberate act. It's an invisibility issue. She wants a foot rub, and you bring flowers. You plan an intimate evening at the opera, and she just needed to hear a sweet commitment that you are her special one. The possibilities for missing the mark are endless. However, if both of you are aware of your languages of love, you can begin to spot acts of love in the other, even if they don't meet your particular needs. She, of course, can do the same for you.

There are ways to get your needs met, and in my estimation, the contract is the forum to negotiate them.

Conclusion

In this chapter, you have developed a different perception about the Lady in your future. You have taken the fantasy and reality that was teased apart, and are now looking for opportunities to practice enjoying fantasy and reality at the same time. You have identified some practices and attitudes that are not desirable, and have self-help books that will assist you in nurturing a future relationship. In addition, every day, you are consciously creating opportunities to serve, which is very effective advertising in your pursuit of a Mistress.

An M/s Studies Book

Chapter Six
Rethink While You Retool

It is important to review the concepts you have learned before you set a goal, devise a plan, and proceed to execute it.

- You can sort Kinky Play into 8 broad categories and have identified those activities that you most wish to do or repeat.
- You can tell the difference between Power Play and Kinky Play.
- You can identify 7 forms of Power Play and select ones that you wish to explore further.
- You have dispelled the myths and negative self-talk that would keep you from being successful.
- You have identified what you don't want in a Mistress.
- You understand what you want in a FemDom and how to communicate with her.
- You will read the following thought process changes with an open mind.

Fantasy vs. Reality

People tend to categorize in extremes. They believe the experience, observable act, idea, or kink should be something that is attainable and reasonable and should be permanently affixed on an imaginary timeline, or it is dismissed as a fantasy. Reality is somehow better than fantasy. Some people even think of men and women whose kinks revolve around fantasy as wannabes, because they do not practice in real time, preferring to stay on the Internet or on the phone.

Worse, we do it to ourselves through our language. Have you ever said, "In your dreams" or "Dream on" to mean that you believe there is no way whatever it is the other person wants is going to happen? It assumes fantasy and reality are opposites, and that reality is better than fantasy.

I want you to open yourself to the concept that fantasy and reality can occupy the same space at the same time. For example, the reality is that my slave is serving my morning coffee. The fantasy that led up to the presentation of that coffee as he kneels before me is his alone. I know it's going on; I allow the time for it, because it enhances our experience together during our daily breakfast. I do not interrupt the process, because it is a ritual of tribute and nothing I can say will be more important than what is happening inside the fantasy in his head. Or, is it the reality? They take up the same space at the same time.

The reality is that my slave sits on the furniture, uses silverware, speaks whenever he wants, and fusses if the eggs are not done to his satisfaction, which is why he prepares them. In reality, I don't particularly care what I eat for breakfast as long as I don't have to cook or wash dishes.

Well, that certainly wasn't very interesting, was it? Of course not. It sounds like the mundane, vanilla life from which we are planning an escape.

However, look at a similar experience through our eyes, and see if the reality of our simple, evening cocktail hour is not enhanced by the fantasy of our power exchange.

I've lost track of time again. It is three minutes to seven. My slave will have my gin gimlet ready. He'll be stuck waiting on his knees until I can get it together enough to arrive at his apartment next door to mine. I drop the laundry into the dryer and hit his front door on a dead run.

The instant I ascend the stairs, my demeanor changes. I am Mistress. I have all the time in the world. Grace and elegance are our creed. Slowly, I turn to face the man who is so powerful, he surrenders to me. He is on his knees, eyes cast downward to the cocktail he has prepared especially for me. We wait. This is our moment together to confirm who and what we are for each other.

He kisses the rim and presents the glass. Then, he gazes into my eyes. This is my favorite time of day. I smile and watch his reaction. He glows. I motion to him to stand, and he escorts me to the library. He seats me, and I offer a toast to our relationship. Then, we pour over whatever article or nonfiction book he has selected while his slave prepares our evening meal.

I watch in silence as each measured step, each action is performed with complete reverence. My breathing becomes deeper, and I cherish his service to me, to us, and to our future.

That was it. That was seven o'clock the way we celebrate it. In reality, nothing happened. Drinks were fixed. Drinks were consumed, and books were read; vanilla activities, and nothing more. However, in our fantasy, we created a world of power exchange and experienced one of many in our day together.

When you are preparing to serve the Dominant Lady of Your Dreams, create moments such as these. No matter how busy she is, or demanding, or pre-occupied, she will see the reverence in your eyes as you complete simple daily tasks for her, and the transformation will be magical.

Today, this very moment, begin to practice meshing your fantasies with your realities and see how easily they become one. Try these exercises:

- Eroticize the normal, whether it is presenting a beverage or laying out her clothing in the morning.
- Segment your day into acts of service and revel in the effect of each one.
- Pretend that special FemDom is with you during your daily activities and respond accordingly. Ladies will notice.
- Journal how you feel about your experience with service.

Keep in mind that none of the above activities assumes you have already captured a Mistress. You are rethinking your reality so you can retool in preparation to serve her. Because the brain can't tell the difference between reality and fantasy, the chemicals emitted are the same, and you benefit from the feelings and physical wellbeing that accompany service in reality, even though it occurred in your imagination.

Another area in which fantasy and reality occupy the same space at the same time is the definition of the relationship. My slave believes I own him. I believe I own him. Therefore, he is owned by me. Period. End of story. It doesn't matter that men are "supposed" to be dominant all of the time or that slaves were emancipated over a hundred years ago. That has nothing to do with what we have worked daily to create.

What about the reality that in current Western society, no one gets to own anyone else? This is a touchy area. My views are not particularly popular and are not defended by current customs. However, I believe the couple who practices Dominance/submission power exchange is a family of equals. They are always equals, which is definitely supported in Western cultures.

It is as important that the slave benefit from the relationship as the Mistress. It is as important that the Mistress grow and learn as it is for the slave to do so. It is equally important for the Dominant Lady to have her needs met as it is for the submissive male to have his met.

How do you create the fantasy of a D/s relationship if you are both equals? The reality is that we are equals and can terminate the relationship at any time. Even strictly drawn-up contracts will not hold up in a court of law. The fantasy is that we will both work hard so that will never need to happen.

In the fantasy, we are not equals, nor do we wish to be. He is my slave, and I am Mistress. As usual in our relationship; the reality and the fantasy take up the same space at the same time.

The key is to negotiate with your Dominant Lady and remain ever vigilant so you have fewer moments of total reality and more of fantasy/reality, which are infinitely more satisfying.

It may not be important that fantasy and reality occupy the same space right now, because you have not captured the Dominant Woman. It is very important, however, to plan ahead so that when you do find her, you will be in the headspace to serve her.

What Do You Bring to the Table?

You look around you, and it seems that everyone has somebody. But, not you. Or, not you right now. There are several reasons why that may be true. You may have family or career responsibilities that keep you from pursuing a Dominant Lady. Your fear of being "outed" may be isolating you. That's the normal fear that people will hate you for being submissive or kinky. Those fears are well-grounded, and when you do land a Mistress, she will appreciate your discretion.

That doesn't help you right now, though. What does help is that you bring to the table a set of experiences, skills and characteristics that, when you do meet her, will allow you to rise above all of the other gentlemen who wish to serve her. It is your responsibility to have on hand a list of those qualifications and a socially acceptable method of "strutting your stuff."

Prepare to serve a Lady in the same manner you would prepare to land the job of your dreams, for in fact, that is what this is. If you were composing a job resumé, would you leave off some of the areas that make you qualified for the position? No, of course you wouldn't. However, that is precisely what frequently happens when male submissives are in the presence of Dommes.

When you are composing a resumé to apply for that special job, it is easy to let self-doubt creep in. *I can't do this. Why would they choose me? I can't pull this off; I don't know why I'm trying.* At some point during the application process, you decide to take the risk and send it in, or you file it in the waste paper basket and feel lousy for the rest of the week.

The same thing happens when you are applying for the position to serve her. Your ego is on the line. As a sidebar, that's a very interesting risk, because once you belong to her, she won't allow you much ego. You may as well get in practice by not listening to Ego over Mistress. She won't be interviewing Ego; she wants to speak with you.

To illustrate, and the Dominant Ladies who will be reading this will have several stories to tell as well, here is how it goes:

John has mastered the concept that fantasy and reality can occupy the same space at the same time. He serves the entire secretarial pool at the office, even though he is a CEO. They find fresh flowers on their desks, his male staff is trained to open doors and seat ladies, and the list goes on. In his mind, the ladies own him, and he takes great pleasure in finding invisible ways to worship them.

Tonight, long after the office has closed for the weekend, John spies Lady Love across the dungeon and is instantly attracted to her. In his imagination, he recreates the scene in which Lancelot professes his love and obedience, essentially his submission, to Guinevere. John is a bard in the local medieval reenactment group of the Society of Creative Anachronism, so he begins to compose a poem to commemorate the moment.

John approaches and stands a respectable distance away, hoping to be recognized. She does, and he approaches, eyes downcast. If he had his way, he'd be on his knees quoting love sonnets from Shakespeare, but he remains mute.

She beckons him to sit at her feet. Dutifully, he kneels in a position that is not comfortable for anyone in the Western world, but looks good, and John desperately wants to look good. He tries not to fidget.

Eyes downcast, he is omitted from the lively conversation she is having with her peers, one that was covered nicely in his undergraduate work at Yale, but he's a submissive, and thinks he should be quiet.

Then, he notices that the hem of her black satin gown is frayed. John knows he could fix that. The tailor who alters his Armani™ suits could do it overnight. Unable to control himself, he wiggles toes in an effort to get some blood to his feet, both of which have fallen asleep, because he'd never really practiced kneeling before.

Lady Love glances down, ruffles John's hair, and asks him to fetch a diet cola with three ice cubes. No spilling. Thrilled at being given an order, he fumbles to his feet and proceeds to follow her direction explicitly. Then he is dumbfounded, unsure of whether or not he should kneel, or kneel and kiss the plastic cup, or kneel and kiss the plastic cup and recite a brief, but romantic poem in iambic pentameter that has appeared full-blown in his mind. But, he misses the opportunity to do anything, and Lady Love, who is now thirsty, simply removes the cup from his hands. Not sure what to do next, John kneels and waits.

Lady Love removes her black satin slipper to reveal a delicate foot with an unimpressive pedicure. He could fix that. Because John's last Mistress was a foot fetishist, John became accomplished at foot worship, as well as grooming. She would look lovely in a special shade of crimson he'd seen last week at the department store.

She places a foot on his thigh, and John picks up the cue to touch. He doesn't want to proceed too quickly, so he performs a basic foot massage and waits to be given the other foot.

Lady Love decides that John is very submissive, wonderfully obedient, and gives a great foot massage. With training, he could probably master foot worship, or at the very least polish her toenails. Unfortunately, he's also nonverbal which means he's probably not well-read or well-educated. The last time she'd tried to teach a submissive to recite poetry, it had been a disaster. It irritates her that he doesn't make eye contact unless requested to do so, so she thinks he may be hiding something. It isn't that he takes away from her; he just doesn't add enough to her life to keep him. Essentially, he's boring. She has enough responsibilities in her life without taking on a boring boy.

Boring? John? I don't think so. Here is an articulate man of considerable wealth who creates medieval fantasies and can quote Shakespeare, not to mention compose in iambic pentameter. He can give pedicures, a service that is out of her budget right now, so she has to muddle by doing her own nails. Unfortunately, Lady Love didn't see any of that. She saw John the way John thought he should appear.

> *Hot tip: Dominant Ladies want interesting partners. Be interesting. Stand out. Give Her a reason to keep you. View every encounter with a Dominant Lady as a job interview. Network. Impress. Get references.*

Compose a resumé. Yes, you read correctly. Write a resumé that will impress the next Almost-Your-Domme who walks into the dungeon. If nothing else, you can list your credentials in the written petition she will probably want before offering you a training collar.

I am one of those Ladies who enjoy having a Dominant at my feet. I like someone who is extremely well-accomplished in his field, is versatile enough to adjust to my world, and entertains me with stimulating, well-informed conversation. That's what turns me on. He can maintain his dominance in all aspects of his life until he comes to me. Then, he's mine, and he will surrender.

But, if he behaves as John did, trying so hard to be the perfect slave that Lady Love lost any interest she may have had in the beginning, it isn't going to work. Lady Love will wonder if there is anyone out there who can give pedicures and write sonnets, and John will go home to his penthouse apartment and wonder why he can't connect with a Mistress.

John completely understood the concept that fantasy and reality could occupy the same space at the same time. What he didn't understand was that in order to share that special space with Lady Love, he had to communicate effectively what he was thinking.

By this time in your life, you probably have a fairly good idea about your own communication skills, including your strengths and weaknesses. Everyone can benefit from ongoing work whether it is in therapy, communication seminars, or reading nonfiction books on the subject. This table is only a suggestion. Use your knowledge and what you are learning to create your own.

COMMUNICATION SKILLS

Skill	Level of Expertise with Dominant Ladies	What am I going to do about it?
Make introductions and initiate conversation	Tongue-tied	Volunteer at a kinky function, so I have a reason to communicate
Maintain interesting conversation		
Request to be of service		
Handle rejection		
Communicate views respectfully when asked		
Listen attentively and actively		
Use body language effectively		
Use facial expressions effectively		
Leave a conversation before you have worn out your welcome		

Resumé

Before you can build a resumé, you need to figure out what you want on yours, in other words, what image you want to project. It's not that you are going to hand it to her immediately, if ever. It's important to have assessed yourself objectively and worked out a plan to accentuate strengths and eliminate weaknesses. If something is not in your control, like a heart problem, you need to have figured out how that is going to be managed to have the least negative impact on your relationship.

Make lists and decide what you want on a resumé. Most of this information will be vanilla. You may be an honest plumber who has earned a top certification in his union. You may be an intelligent deputy who has retired on a pension.

- Strengths
  What are my best character traits?
  What can I do? What are my skills?
  What are my accomplishments?
  What can I do to please a Mistress?

- Weaknesses
  What are my worst character traits?
  What do I need to learn to be successful with a FemDom?
  What are the things in my life I'm ashamed of?
  What do I do that I know will not please a Mistress?

- What I Can't Change, But Will Manage
  Health concerns
  Family obligations
  Time and money obligations
  Pick your own problem

Your strengths will probably be easily recognized. Your weaknesses are what you've been hiding. Tease apart the problem and devise ways to minimize or eradicate a weakness. Manage the areas you know will cause problems in the next relationship. Use your lists to make a chart in the next chapter.

Asset vs. Liability

How do you make yourself an asset and not a liability? It really isn't that difficult, unless you are truly a liability, and then you'll have to work on that until you are ready to serve her.

She will decide if you are an asset or a liability based upon the plus/minus columns she's rating. Are you more trouble than you are worth? Do you have more baggage than she does? Are you needier than she is? Are the great times worth the irritation of the day-in-day-out living with you?

Become an asset by taking care of business and minimizing your liabilities. In other words, if your life revolves around your dog, decide what you are going to do with Fluffy when your Mistress summons you. If you know you're a workaholic, make sure you've planned ahead so someone can take over when you take the Lady of your Dreams to Hedonism II.

If your best friends tell you that you are too critical, prepare yourself to be more accepting in her presence. Practice the art of letting go. Whatever it is that makes you right is not as important as cementing a relationship with a perfect Domme.

On the other side of the coin is recognizing whether a Mistress is more of a liability or more of an asset in your life. Try not to foster a relationship with anyone who has more problems than you do. If she has an ailing mother who is going to require long-term care, be prepared for it. If the Special Lady is divorcing a Neanderthal, but she still loves him, give her a rain check. When she gets her life figured out, she can let you know.

On the one hand, you need to place your life first. You need to be the healthy one. After that, you can consider a symbiotic relationship in which both of you are better for it or a synergistic one in which neither of you could reach the incredible heights without the other.

Be careful that one or the other of you does not reach parasitic status. No one wants to live with a parasite. This is the Mistress who lives for you and only for you. She is jealous of your time away from her. She indicates that you aren't a real male submissive if you don't (pick your own activity.) If you find yourself acting and thinking in a manner that you wouldn't have embraced as a single slave-in-waiting, chances are it will be a short term relationship. There is nothing wrong with short-term relationships unless one or both parties are convinced it was going to be a long-term one.

Time Allotted to the Task

In reading this book, you have expanded your knowledge and rethought the kinky activities in which you wish to participate. You have separated Kinky Play from Power Exchange and have selected styles and levels that appeal to you. You have dispelled the myths and the negative self-talk. You are better able to identify a Dominant Lady, and you have a clear concept on how to get along with her. Congratulate yourself in that you are making strides in preparing to serve the Lady of your fantasy, as well as the Lady of your reality.

You may need to review some of the previous sections, if you cannot clearly state what you have learned. You may need to edit what you've written. Perhaps you've had an epiphany. Now is the time to revamp your new outlook before investing any time in a model that has too many flaws or is hastily thrown together.

It's true that most gentlemen do not pursue a Lady while armed with a business and marketing plan, but by creating one, you will have an edge on the competition. The next part is more difficult because it requires committing resources, including money and time.

One reason quality gentlemen do not have the Dominant Lady of their dreams is because they don't allot the time it takes to capture her. That's right. Capture. She isn't going to be your Goddess just because you want one. She knows you want one; she just isn't sure she's the Goddess for you.

If men spent one half the amount of time actively pursuing a Mistress as they do masturbating about one, the world would be a happier place.

Prioritizing Strengths, Weaknesses and Situations You Can't Change

We all understand the priority challenges that we face in our daily lives. Which problem gets your attention? Why? Do you pick the tough ones or the easy ones first?

Because you are almost ready to set goals and objectives in your plan to capture a Mistress, it is important to accept the priorities in your life and be willing to accept the ones in hers. One or both of you has children. Or, elderly parents. Or, a job that requires you to travel. Or, you work late hours. Or, one or the other of you has made a commitment that takes time away from the relationship both of you are invested in: church, clubs, school, job, computer games, volunteerism, sports, etc. Priority challenges are a threat to the relationship you are creating with her unless you manage them. Know that through compromise and planning, your dreams can come true.

Until you are in negotiation with a Special Lady, you will need to create an interesting and fulfilling life for yourself. Frankly, she isn't interested in a boy doll that has been sitting on the shelf waiting for the perfect Domme to open the closet door.

Once you find her, be ready to accept the opportunity costs of having your dreams come true. One or both of you may need to cut back on activities that were pleasurable when you were alone. If this is not very palatable, consider negotiating for release time to pursue the priority alone. Nothing is being taken away from you. What you have with your Mistress is vastly different than what you have with the rest of the world. The better you both understand this, the better the chance of creating a long-term power exchange.

Plan ahead, accept that there will be problems and predict what they may be so you have a better chance of creating mutually acceptable solutions.

Conclusion

In this chapter, you examined your strengths, your weaknesses and identified the situations in your life you cannot control. By taking a serious look at them, you can create a viable plan, including a resumé, in order to capture your Mistress.

An M/s Studies Book

Chapter Seven
Plan for Success

Use the list from the previous chapter and create a chart of your own. List several strengths you feel you possess. Be sure to identify at least three from each strength category.

STRENGTHS

Strength	Why is it an asset?	How can I use it?	How can I advertise it?	Who will want it?
Trait: Reliable	I keep my promises.	I will meet deadlines.	I will say, "You can count on me" every time I agree to help.	FemDoms and their friends
Skill: Computer repair	Fem/Doms have computers.	I can serve her by installing a hard drive.	I can offer services at the next BDSM social.	FemDoms and their friends who own computers
Skill: Computer Engineer	I earn a higher salary.	I can find work if I relocate.	I can wear a class ring or a college sports shirt.	FemDoms who have a higher education filter

To please her: Foot massage	Fem/Doms work hard and have sore feet.	An excuse for contact, I can sit at her feet and offer.	I can admire her shoes and feet.	FemDoms who value service or are foot fetishists

By understanding what your strengths are, how you can use them and how you can let others know you have them, you are better able to attract a Mistress by making it through her filters. FemDoms are not mind readers. We need your input.

Now, repeat the same process with your personal weaknesses. Create your own chart. Focus on the top two weaknesses in each category. Listing too many will make it too hard to turn any weaknesses into strengths.

WEAKNESSES

Weakness	Why is it a weakness?	What will I do about it?	By when?	How will I let her know I'm working on it?
Trait: Slovenly	She won't let me live with her.	Spend 10 minutes a night picking up and cleaning.	I'll start after I get back from the convention.	I'll tell her when it is appropriate in the conversation.

Skill: My table manners aren't good.	She won't let me to eat with her.	I'll read a book on table etiquette and practice.	I'll pick up 3 new skills by the first of the month.	I'll go to the social and use good table manners.
Ashamed: I hate my dad.	I won't take her to meet my family.	I'll begin counseling.	I'll start when I get the raise next month.	I'll tell her before signing a training contract.
Not pleasing Mistress: I spend too much on sex sites.	I won't have as much money to take her out to eat or buy toys.	I will reduce the amount of money spent to fit my budget.	I'll do it when I find a FemDom and think it's serious	I won't unless she asks.

By understanding and accepting your weaknesses, you can manage them. Some will disappear, because you have taken the steps to neutralize them. Some won't go anywhere, because you like them. I have a weakness in that I am blunt. I recognize it. I know how to be tactful. Frequently, I choose not to be.

Repeat the same process with situations that could become or are currently a problem. Create your own chart. List the most important problems and brainstorm several solutions before picking one or two for each problem.

It is never appropriate to misrepresent a situation by sidestepping the issue or indicating that it in some way will not be important if it really is. Many ladies require full disclosure, or completely divulging all information in a truthful manner. Discovering after the fact that there is a major situation that will adversely affect her time with you is one of the quickest ways to find yourself without a Mistress.

SITUATION

Situation	Why could it be a problem?	What can I do to minimize it?	When do I tell her?
Health: I have an old football injury.	I can't kneel for more than a minute or two.	I will figure out a way to sit at her feet.	I'll tell her before I need to kneel.
Family: I'm a non-custodial parent.	I have the kids every other weekend.	I can make family time special and Mistress time special.	I'll tell her when she asks me to go with her on a weekend.
Time: I'm on call a lot.	Mistress can't count on me to be with her.	I will make sure she has an escort to take my place.	I will tell her the first time she asks me to go somewhere with her.
Money: I'm paying alimony.	I don't have the money to pay for everything.	I will negotiate paying for 60% of the entertainment.	I will tell her when she invites me to an event I cannot afford.

Many of our situations are long-term, as in custodial arrangements, or cannot be changed markedly, as in having a seizure disorder. By fully understanding the impact the situation can have on the relationship with a FemDom, you are better able to minimize the negative effects. In addition, projecting yourself as a problem solver is very attractive. Dominant women like to be in control, but they may not want to think for the submissive partner.

At this point, if you have been honest when creating the charts, you are ready to make yourself more attractive to the FemDom, who is wondering why it is taking you so long to find her. Everyone can improve themselves. Men who are learning and striving to be better are more attractive than meek gentlemen who are patiently waiting for someone to notice them.

In this next chart, create a plan for growth. It needs to be detailed enough to realize what steps must be taken. It needs to have an outcome, so you can chart your progress. At some point in your relationship with your new Lady, you may want to show her how hard you have been working to prepare for the time when she will let you serve her.

GROWTH PLAN

Objective	Plan	Evaluation
I will improve my cooking skills.	1) This fall I will save $400. 2) Next spring, I will take night classes in Italian cuisine. 3) I will attend 90% of the classes and complete all of the assignments. 4) I will include the ingredients in my food budget. 5) I will cook a full meal once per week to perfect my skills. 6) I will take additional classes as necessary.	Upon completion of the class, I will bring an Italian entreé to all work functions that require a dish. Once every six weeks, I will host a small dinner party.
I will improve my wardrobe.	1) I will increase the clothing/dry cleaning allowance in the budget. 2) I will buy magazines and pay attention to trends. 3) I will seek advice on color and style. 4) Within six months, I will create one new outfit to project my new image. 5) I will care for the clothing appropriately.	I will wear my new clothing at an appropriate event. I will accept compliments like a gentleman.
I will improve my communication skills with women.	1) I will read 2 self-help books about relationships. 2) I will practice in the workplace. 3) I will seek female friendships. 4) I will compliment others.	Within six months, I will ask a Dominant Lady out to coffee.

Conclusion

It's time to write a resumé, one very different from the last one you created to get your job. There are as many ways to write this as there people writing them.

This is the shortest chapter in the book, yet it probably took the longest time to digest. You've analyzed the charts and taken the time to fill out your own charts from the appendix. By naming your strengths, your weaknesses, the situations you cannot control, you can use them to your advantage. You have a resumé which helps you see the path you need to take on this wonderful journey. You have begun your growth plan, and you have discovered just how much time it takes to make your dreams come true.

An M/s Studies Book

Chapter Eight
Work the Plan

Fish Where the Fish Are

I consistently hear that there are no available Dominant Women in the world. Every other FemDom they know is already attached in a monogamous relationship. As a sidebar, I think that monogamy is one of the worst ideas man has originated, right along with nuclear holocaust.

Then, I ask the gent where he's been looking for the ladies. Well, he usually confesses that he hasn't. He's been waiting for them to notice him. Notice him doing what? Where? How does that work?

If you want a Dominant Lady, present yourself with dignity and elegance in places where they congregate. At the local BDSM organization, try volunteering. Many of us are exhausted from trying to do everything for everyone. What we wouldn't give for a gentleman of quality and submission to take a little of the work off our hands! Volunteer.

If you are uncertain of where to find a BDSM organization, do an Internet search. Sign up for e-mail lists so you get to know the folks before attending a kinky party or seminar. Buy a copy of **Power Exchange**, an alternative lifestyle magazine that lists nearby organizations and when they have their events.

If you are going to a Baptist revival, chances are that the pickings will be slim for Dominant Women. Not that they aren't there, but they won't be in the headspace to find you. You will be invisible, and so will they.

Find a book club. Women love to read. Nothing is hotter than a submissive gent who wants to read the next Oprah recommendation at the feet of his special Lady. It gets my heart beating faster just thinking about it. Of course, my family spends the evenings reading the dictionary. To each his own.

Take a class at the local community college. It doesn't matter what it is; just pick one that is primarily female and in the age group that interests you. Call the registrar to make sure there are ample candidates. I personally recommend classes that require you to journal. Ladies love a man who can write. Or develop computer savvy. A self-help class is great, too. I think I fell in love with my slave when he replaced the dimmer switches.

Even better, teach a community college course that Dominant Ladies would take. I'm not sure what that would be, but Single Ladies and the Art of Auto Maintenance comes to mind. Once you have established that you are their guru, you can serve coffee and praise them for whatever it is that creeps into your submissive, deviant mind.

Take advantage of social stereotypes. If you have any skills associated with masculinity, parade them proudly. There isn't a Dominant Female out there who doesn't appreciate a man who can repair a weed-eater. Service is hot, very hot. If you are skilled, you may want to advertise in the local paper: Handyman who wishes to serve that special lady who knows her own mind… height and weight appropriate, of course. If you are one of those lucky guys who likes Big, Beautiful Women, that's all the better. Heaven knows there are enough of us to go around.

My point here is that if you want a Dominant Lady, you have to figure out where they are, plan an attack, and execute it without the Lady knowing what it is that you are trying to accomplish. It isn't that difficult. Most of us are so over obligated, we don't notice the gent until he's on top of us (oops, poor choice of words.)

Try filling out the chart below. If you find it difficult, perhaps you need to develop some new skills or interests.

SKILLS

Skills I possess	Where can I show it off in the kink world?	Where can I show it off in the vanilla world?
Carpet laying	Volunteer to lay carpet at the local dungeon	Volunteer to teach a free one-day seminar at the community center as a Self-Help for Singles

CPR	Volunteer to teach at a Dungeon	Assist teaching first aid to workshop partici-pants
Electrical wiring	Assist in a toy making workshop on TENS units or electro-stim	Volunteer to teach basics to a singles group

Narrowing the Search Too Early

Create filters that a real, live person can get through. You wouldn't walk into a financial planning office armed with a portfolio containing the only funds you would consider and an ultimatum if they don't give them to you. Of course not. The same goes for finding a Domme.

> *Hot Tip: The FemDom you've been fantasizing about since you were eighteen doesn't live on this planet.*

Ladies who notice your skills are not going to care how accomplished you are if you aren't accepting of them as people first and FemDoms second.

Decide early on whether you are looking for your Fantasy Mate or simply a Dominant Lady who can fulfill your dreams with energy and hard work on both your parts. Sure, we all have filters. That's how we screen out the crazy people from our best friends.

However, sometimes, when we have these incredibly well developed, specific fantasies about the Lover of our Dreams, we have narrowed the search to the point that only fictional characters meet our qualifications. Ask any lady who has joined a Hundred Club, which means she's watched the same movie a hundred times.

* Hot tip: If you meet a charter member of a Hundred Club, watch her video to figure out why she'd sit over 200 hours in front of the same video. Chances are you've knocked on the door of her fantasy. Even if you can't replicate it, you can certainly re-create a few choice moments from the movie to please her.

If you are realistic and have relegated the Perfect 10 to your fantasies, are you trapped by the "one true Domme" myth followed by the "one true sub" myth? Until it comes up, she's the one you are with, and all the time you have is now. Whatever time she spends with other submissives or play partners does not take away from the precious time she spends with you. If it did, she wouldn't be spending any time with you at all.

Are you bound by the "height-weight appropriate" double standard? So what if she's overweight, either by a little or a lot? If you think you are going to be servicing her in bed, it may be an issue for you if you cannot perform with a heavier Lady, but the perception of beauty changes over time and as the relationship deepens. It would be a terrible waste to miss an opportunity because you do not have an appreciation of big, beautiful women. Yet.

Strip down and take a look in the mirror. Would you want her to dismiss you because of your appearance? Of course not. Even if you are a stud with a six-pack in the abs department, she may be into big, hairy men, or boyish Asian men, or (pick your own description as long as it is something that you aren't.) If she is willing to broaden her search, it may behoove you to do the same.

I'm not asking you to forfeit your fantasy, just broaden it a little to include ladies who actually exist in this world and may be living in your neighborhood and taking that class on pedicures you want to attend.

Are you enslaved by the "two or more years younger than me" hidden criteria? Somewhere in our past, probably around the time of our first high school prom, we accepted the confining idea that the best relationships are between people who are close in age. We are supposed to have more in common or some such foolishness.

Then, for whatever reason, when a man reaches his forties, women under thirty become fascinating and desirable. Not that they aren't, but these are stereotypes to be examined. I'm in my fifties and have no difficulty maintaining vibrant, interesting power exchange relationships with gentleman much younger and much older than me. I have something these gentlemen want. Dominance. My age becomes invisible as the relationship progresses.

The exception is when age is integral to the fantasy or power exchange. For some, they cannot submit unless there is a difference or a similarity in age. Don't change the requirements you need most.

Next, there is the "perfect body syndrome." You don't have one; why should she? Yes, if you are going to create the perfect masturbation fantasy, imagine a "10". However, a "7" may be the one who is willing to put up with your less than perfect physique in exchange for the honor of being served by you.

It isn't who you can find. It's what you can create. Otherwise, you are simply looking for a needle in a haystack. As long as you enjoy the search, that's fine. If you are seriously planning to have a Dominant Lady in your life, it would behoove you to invest in a metal detector before you attack the next haystack.

Try the chart below and determine where you need to improve.

IMPROVING PERCEPTIONS

Narrow perceptions that I can broaden	How can I broaden them?
My Domme must be taller than me.	She can be a few inches shorter than me, and I'll buy her heels.
I need a Mistress with at least a 38DD.	And I'm willing to pay for the surgery.
The Lady must live within 35 minutes of my apartment.	I will consider taking a commuter flight to visit her.
She has to be monogamous and heterosexual.	She can have other play partners, but just not when we are together.

Advertise!

First impressions are everything. No, ladies shouldn't judge you that quickly. However, they do, and that's the way it is, so use that tip to your advantage. Dress to attract the person you want.

Dress to impress. It doesn't get any clearer than that. If you want Ginger Rogers, take lessons in ballroom dancing, a lot of them and frequently. Overdress for all occasions. If you want a Goddess, go to nude resorts and get certified in massage therapy. If you want a Biker Bitch, get motorcycle boots and preferably, a motorcycle. She'll notice if you don't have one. Yakking about the cycle you had in college won't cut it.

I personally like class in dress. I prefer the fifties look. Elegant ladies wearing seamed stockings and girdles. I enjoy teaching a gentleman to dress me. Or, even better, let me put the apron on him. This doesn't apply to all men, just the ones I want. How do I find them?

I ask. If they look at me like I'm crazy, I figure they aren't the ones to put on my stockings that night.

> *Hot Tip: If you aren't sure what to wear, choose black. Lots of black. Not that black is an especially dominant or submissive color, but it is hard to advertise to anyone you are into power exchange wearing a pocket protector and a pastel shirt.*

I took a friend of mine to the outlet mall to do a "makeover."

He's generous, brilliant and has a devotion to music that could be termed reverent. He's also a very large man, so we found a store specializing in men who are big and tall. An engineer, he is fashion-challenged, as well as size-challenged. Once the clerk, who was "co-topping" him in what he described later as a nonconsensual setup, had the correct size, we smothered him in grey, black and dark shirts with matching ties. He even picked out a pair of suspenders. He looked fantastic, dapper actually, and his new clothing allowed him to attract a submissive lady who loves the opera almost as much as he does.

> *Hot Tip First impressions: You only get one.*

The same is true for submissive males. Dress as the counterpart for the Lady you wish to serve. If you want Guinevere, search the consignment shops for a poet shirt. If you want to be an ashtray, get a gold-plated lighter and sit in the smoking section. You get the idea.

The time to act is now. Figure out what you want her to be, imagine yourself as her perfect counterpart, and then find clothing and accessories to advertise your kink and your availability. Look your best at all times, whatever that is. Your best may be jeans and cowboy boots. That's fine, if you want her to dress like Dale Evans. You can be her Roy Rogers, and everybody is happy.

The problem occurs when you find a Lady who dresses differently than you usually do. Then, you have to decide. Do you try to attract her with a totally different style of clothing? Or, do you attempt to please her by pairing your costuming to hers? If you can do it without sacrificing too much of who you are, try to please her.

I don't care if you have the hottest leather harness and matching blindfold in the confines of your personal dungeon. If you present to me with frayed jeans and a poor manicure, I'm not going to be as receptive as I would if your shoes were shined. Perhaps I'm in the minority of a minority, but why take the chance?

If you aren't searching for me, wear the frayed jeans and wrinkled shirt. Who knows? You may attract your counterpart out there somewhere assuming she is a sixties, free-love kind of Gal.

Warning: If you fantasize about a rubber-clad Goddess, chances are she will ignore you in cotton anyway. Get a rubber arm band or watch band or go all out and invest in a rubber or Latex shirt. Advertise yourself.

Try filling in the blanks and then go to the mall. If you already have a FemDom in mind, ask her to assist you in a makeover. Even if you don't become partners, I guarantee you'll become friends. Gentlemen who know more Dommes, meet more Dominant Ladies.

Fill in the blanks to help you understand the relationship between how you look and how you feel:

I like to wear _____, because it makes me feel _____. The Lady I want to attract will see me and

think _____. I like her to wear _____,
because it makes me feel _____. I can
serve her when she wears it, because _____.

> * *Hot tip: If you really want her to wear a garment, nails or a hair*
> *style, offer to pay for it or present her with a gift certificate.*

Case in point: My slave adores semi-formal dining in military fetish. Unfortunately, I'm a nudist who wears clothing primarily because I get cold. My interest in stalking eBay™ for that perfect 1942 Canadian nurse mess dress uniform is minimal. However, since it's gorgeous, and since he purchased it for me, I wear it frequently. I know it pleases him. He thinks I'm beautiful.

Let's take a quick look at beauty. I'm in my fifties. I've had a mastectomy with no reconstruction. I'm short. My tummy is getting out of control. I have absolutely gorgeous feet and nails, which, to my knowledge, my slave has never noticed. He's a cunt guy. Until he brought it up, I didn't know how attractive mine was. Beauty is not only culturally defined, it is fetish defined. Whatever you've liked since you understood your sexuality, is what is beautiful. Find it. Buy it. Present it as a gift. Make sure she understands it is part of who you are, and she, if she's smart, will wear it proudly.

The same goes for you. I don't care how you feel about it, if she reads historical romance novels and thinks a Scottish kilt is hot, you'd better wrap your head around liking to wear one. Hers is the only opinion that matters. If you can't hide the fact that you think you look stupid in a kilt, offer the gift to her as a symbol of your submission. Watch her eyes, and you may decide the kilt looks great.

There is a fine line between making a good impression and lying. You have a responsibility to contract law's Truth in Advertising. A Dominant Lady has an accurate bullshit-meter she calibrates each time a potential slave enters her domain. Be honest. Borrowing your brother-in-law's 50-foot yacht is vastly different than owning it yourself. That you borrowed it for her is an act of service, which she will appreciate. That you do not own it and want her to believe that you do, is not. She is more interested about who you really are than what you can fabricate.

* Hot tip: If you lie and get caught, do not expect her to punish you and later offer forgiveness as you grovel at her feet with a hard-on the size of Michigan's Upper Peninsula. Expect her to order you from her presence and tell her Dominant friends what a creep you are.

There is a difference between creating a new and fascinating world of power exchange with the Domme of your Dreams and making up stuff to jockey for a better position with her. I have never met a FemDom who did not appreciate honesty. She's a leader, but she has to know who is following. You may as well tell her the truth up front, because it won't take her long to figure it out anyway.

On the other hand, you are not responsible for misconceptions she has derived all by herself. These usually fall into the category of myths that she assumed were mutually believed. Her mantra may be, "You are her one true sub. You will love only her. You love her no matter how crazy or abusive she is." These are not necessarily parameters you have agreed to in the relation-ship. When you negotiate, speak and write clearly, and you will minimize some of these deal breakers.

Try filling out the chart. Set a deadline to go to the mall and find the clothing you need.

IMPRESSIONS

I want her to see me as (a):	So, I will wear:	Do I currently own what I need?	Where and how will I get it?
Sissy maid	a French maid costume	no	http://sissyland. com by the first of next month
Refined	A dark suit, the best I can afford, with new shoes	I own shoes. I need a new black suit.	I will watch the sales and buy one after the holidays.
Country Western dancer	Cowboy boots	Yes, but they need to be resoled and shined.	I'll take the boots in to be resoled and shined on Tuesday.

Niche Marketing

How do you rise above all of the other fascinating, gifted submissives who are your competition? You create a niche and move in. Let the Ladies come to you.

It is not your challenge to compete against all other submissive males in the Western Hemisphere. It is your challenge to create a niche market that will attract the type of Dominant Lady with whom to form that special attachment.

For example, I like foot worship. It piques my interest every time a gentleman brings it up. To advertise, I wear my toenails longer than is fashionable and wear open-toed stylish pumps. My pedicure is current, and the red polish bold. I'm advertising.

I would be interested in a gent who enjoys foot worship and can perform. Many men can give great a foot massage, but there is a difference when a male eroticizes the foot. If the gentleman finds feet incredibly sexy, but doesn't know what to do to please the Lady whose foot he's holding, he has a different problem. I would prefer to teach the man specific ways to please me, not to recreate the wheel and show him how to polish nails. In other words, I would like to instruct holding the polish wand between his teeth, not the differences between the hardness and long lasting qualities of nail polish. If he has gleaned it off the Internet or in basic classes, he is more valuable to me and worth the time it takes to train.

In your case, become an expert. Ladies enjoy knowledgeable men. Think of an activity that excites you and learn something about it every day. Keep notes. Write a book, and let me edit it. That would certainly be good advertising, wouldn't it? You get the idea.

Within a short period, you will probably have exhausted much of what there is to learn on a topic, if you make it specific. Expand your knowledge to take classes in your kink, either from your local BDSM organization or from the vanilla world that doesn't know you are planning to present that special Lady with a full body massage, including aromatherapy. Eventually, offer to teach a BDSM workshop or mentor another. These are all good advertising strategies.

Then, if you're lucky, and if you're really good, you'll attract the Dominant Ladies, and it won't take as much work to find them.

As an example, my slave is fascinated by cunts, a word I had always found appalling and ill bred. However, when he says it with such reverence, I believe my mons, labial folds, clitoris and vagina are exactly what he says they are… a beautiful cunt.

My slave also enjoys nature photography. By combining cunt worship and photography, he created a niche market doing what he loves: filming cunts in flower motifs. See www.photosbycorwin.com. Eventually, he had enough fun for an erotic art book. He has no shortage of models, because he has created a niche, and he makes every lady feel beautiful.

Create your own niche. It doesn't matter if you are clueless and uneducated about what excites you. Set the path toward becoming an expert. If you don't have any ideas at this point, masturbate. I'm serious. Take an index card and summarize what turns you on.

Next, brainstorm, or make an extensive list upon which you show no judgment, about all of the possible skills you could learn that would enhance your time together with this elusive, FemDom. If nothing else, it will improve your fantasies.

Prioritize the list according to your own criteria. Let's pretend that Wine Steward skills are at the top of your list. If you are short of funds, it may be difficult to procure that special bottle of wine that has aged longer than you have and has come from a vineyard located in a part of the world you can't find on a map. None of this is a problem, because you are going to approach it in small, achievable steps.

Attend inexpensive wine tasting classes or offer to serve at such occasions in exchange for learning about fine wines. Get creative. Involve friends who may have knowledge about wine you don't possess. Get a part time job at a winery, even if it's weeding. Find people who love wine. The only thing they like as much as wine is talking about wine. People who have lots of wine, love wine. They may not mind sharing a sip with you along with their knowledge.

Keep a log or create a photo journal about the experiences you have had learning about wine. Present it to your Lady who will undoubtedly appreciate a demonstration of your devotion and servitude even before you met her. That's hot.

Maybe Wine Steward isn't your niche. No problem. Create your own niche. Make it a reality. Journal it. Present it to the Lady of your Dreams.

A word of caution: Ladies respect a gentleman who is fiscally responsible. Don't select polo as your niche if you can't afford it. Once you fill out the chart below, create a financial plan that will allow you to achieve a niche market.

CREATING A NICHE MARKET

My niche, even if I don't know much now	What I need to learn	How I can demonstrate mastery
Italian cuisine	Gourmet cooking, serving	Invite the FemDom and her friend to a special luncheon
Wine and cheese parties	Wine, cheese, serving	Serve at a local BDSM party
Valet service	To drive a standard shift	Serving at parties

Sell Yourself

There is a difference between advertising and selling. I'm not sure what it is, but this is my book, and I'll define it in terms we understand. Advertising is projecting an image that you believe is favorable to getting your needs met. You can advertise all you want, but if no one is watching, you won't be successful. You will be accomplished, but alone.

Selling is using advertising and anything else you can come up with to persuade that new FemDom that you are the one she should choose. As part of your campaign, you are going to have available to you your entire resumé of skills. Don't write them down and give them to her, but do keep them close to you so they can appear in a conversation if the opportunity arises. Who knows? Your newest skill may be cha-cha, and perhaps she's always wanted to dance.

I think you could probably read any good sales book and apply it to the kink world. The author may be teaching you to sell a car. The author will never know that you are now the car.

This is a good analogy, because if you want to sell a car, you don't list all of the rotten things that happened to the car or what's wrong with it now. You present the good points about the car and answer honestly about its less than sterling qualities. You are a car, and it is your job to advertise yourself on the lot.

You are also the car salesman which offers a bit more detachment. Pretend to sell yourself to the Mistress, but do it through an honest car salesman's point of view.

You have the opportunity to change the way the world views you and most especially, the way you view yourself. Today, as of this very moment, you are a submissive male, the perfect mate for one or more Dominant Ladies. So what if your first wife thinks you're slovenly, a poor lover, or (choose your own derogatory characteristic?) Your new Mistress isn't going to know any of this unless you tell her. Project what you want others to believe, and they will.

The most beneficial outcome from this type of thinking is that it becomes true for you. If you believe you are attractive, you begin to diet and exercise to maintain those qualities. If you want to project servitude, you hold doors open for women who have never given you a glance… until now.

As a warning note, try not to view yourself in ways only a mentally deranged Dominatrix would believe. If you have bad knees, don't portray yourself as a marathon runner. Don't offer to kneel at her feet all evening. Try something more credible that plays to your strengths. I'm sure there is a fine line between selling and delusion. I think that if it's successful, it's selling. If it's not, it's probably delusion.

SKILLS AND ADVERTISING

Skills worth advertising	The skill makes me feel:	Projecting the image
Landscaping architect	Useful, productive, entrepreneurial, servile	Competent, creative, service oriented, self-less
Web Designer	Creative, entrepreneurial	Helpful, supportive
eBay™ Store Tutor	Creative, entrepreneurial	Needed, competent

Now, consider some of your deficit areas and turn them into salable commodities. Let's go back to the football knee that keeps you from kneeling at her feet for hours on end. So what if you can't kneel? You can sit at her feet with your hands positioned in a manner of servitude. She'll understand it. Others who see you will understand it. Kneeling is a fabrication of the Internet and doesn't translate well with Western society. Embrace what you can do.

SOLUTIONS TO LIMITATIONS

I can't:	Therefore I will:	And it will be perceived that:
Stand for long periods because I have a bad back	Seat my Lady when-ever possible, sit or lay at her feet	I am pleasing her, I am submissive to her
Spend a lot of money on dining out	Create fabulous meals for her in her home on my budget	I am attentive, creative and appreciate our time together
See her on the first, third or fifth weekends of the month	Make the second and fourth weekends as special as possible	I am a good father to my non-custodial chil-dren. I treasure the time with her.

Online vs. Real Time Relationships

I have online dating to thank for my smooth entrance into the BDSM community and most especially to a gentleman who understood that although I viewed myself as the ultimate submissive slave, I wasn't. Online, I could maintain that Gorean persona that had Dominant men wooing/capturing me. In person, it didn't hold up very well. Kneeling and remaining silent in high protocol wasn't as much fun in person as it was online. My expressions betray what I'm thinking, and that's never a good thing.

That doesn't make real time more "right" than online relationships. They are simply different forms of power exchange with different rules. Recently, I found out an online friend had passed away suddenly from a heart attack. I remembered her in her thirties in the chat rooms, but she was really seventy-five. She was a very convincing younger woman, and I do not begrudge her the creation of a persona that gave her a life vastly different from the one she endured. I'm not saying it's ethical to purposefully give misinformation to those whom you believe are being truthful. I'm saying it is not such a horrible thing, either. Online is simply its own special kind of fantasy.

I meet many, many people at the local BDSM functions who met online, fell in love and are in the process of living happily ever after. They couldn't have achieved that without honesty in the chat rooms, at least I don't think they could.

Most of us also have a horror story in which the same set-up resulted in a completely different outcome. The one that comes to mind for me was in Dallas when I had convinced an experienced FemDom to accompany me on my first liason with a real live foot fetishist. When the gentleman arrived at the hotel ready to play, I realized he was at least 20 years older than his online advertisement stated. In addition, he hadn't done the preparation to learn how to operate the foot bath he'd brought.

It was almost comic watching the three of us try to resurrect a foot worship scene by reading the directions on how to assemble a foot bath. In the end, we shook hands and sent the gentleman on his way with no scene. You know, I have nothing against playing with older men. My slave is ten years my senior. However, I do have a problem with establishing an online relationship and then having that information change markedly when I meet the gent in person. It's my bullshit-meter that registers betrayal when that happens.

Consequently, I tell the truth, primarily because I can't remember lies very well. I'm a phone dominatrix. My pictures do not show my face to facilitate fantasy. Consequently, the client will frequently ask my age. As of this writing, it's fifty-three. I'm barely five feet tall, but I can play an Amazon if that is what the scene calls for, especially since I only have one breast. I always ask if the gent wants the truth, and he needs to understand he'll get it. I am not responsible for his emotions and judgment surrounding my honesty.

You are the only one who can draw the line between fantasy and reality in online vs. real time relationships. Take a serious look at yourself in the following chart:

CREATE A LIFE ONLINE

In real life, I'm:	But online, I could be:	So:
Really dominant at work and run a large company	Submissive in the chat room or maybe even a slave	I'll learn how to type my name in lower-case and address FemDoms so they will invite me to sit at their feet
Self-conscious about being naked	Naked and chained	I'll practice by sleeping nude
Physically weak	Muscle bound	I'll go to the gym and lift weights twice a week

Behaviors that Advertise

Before you have an opportunity to share your submissive journey with prospective FemDoms, you will have to get their attention. Practice excellent manners, and you have a good chance.

Find a BDSM organization and go to one of their meetings. No, you probably aren't a joiner. No, you probably won't find your Dream Domme the first night. No, you probably won't be the center of attention. Remember: people are watching, and if you present well, they will help you. We all know a Domme who needs a really fine submissive in her life.

- Follow all rules of the host or the host organization. That includes being truthful on any papers you are asked to sign. Frequently, an organization will ask that the real name be given along with proof of identification, usually in the form of a driver's license.

If you are concerned about the security of the document, ask. They will tell you, and you can decide if you wish to sign or not. Organizations insist on identification to protect themselves and to protect you. If you choose not to sign, excuse yourself politely and leave.

- As you are signing in, explain that you are new and ask for assistance. Some organizations have greeters, volunteers that welcome newcomers. Other groups have an orientation meeting that explains some of the rules that may not at first be obvious. Most educational organizations are not dating services. Don't ask about that. There will be plenty of time to figure out how couples link up later.

- If you are attending a munch, or BDSM social, at a restaurant, order food. The establishment sponsors the kinky organization only as long as they attract paying customers. This is also a good excuse to openly offer to refill beverages.

- Stand a respectful distance from any conversation that does not include you. Look at ease and alert to an opportunity to serve. Keep your hands behind you, your legs spread at shoulder's width, attentive. Do not, for any reason, kneel. Perhaps some-one else is kneeling, but you aren't. Reserve is better than incorrect behavior. Should a Lady ask you to kneel at her feet, accept graciously. It's good advertising.

- Sit on furniture, but rise immediately if a Dominant enters and there are not enough seats. Sit erect and be attentive. No slouching. Offer to help put chairs away when the meeting is over.

- Walk slowly and with dignity. Do not hurry, especially if you have been given a task. It is better to act decisively and with purpose, attending to every element of the request.

- Eat where and what the other submissives are eating. If they are served at a separate table, go there. You have as much a right to be there as those who have already found the perfect Dom. Do not overfill your plate. Use utensils only if you see other submissives doing so. Use fine table manners, including eating slowly. Do not finish eating before the Dominants.

- Find opportunities to serve. Offer to assist the person in charge of dinner, beverages or appetizers. If someone refuses to speak to you, chances are he or she is in high protocol and does not have a voice. If you are lucky enough to be chosen to assist, serve equally, not just the incredibly hot FemDoms on the patio. Frequently, better references can be awarded by those of us who are more experienced.
- Carry anything of anybody's, if they will let you. Offer respectfully. Say something like, "Sir, may I assist you with those bags, Sir?" Be of assistance to the male Doms, and the FemDoms will take it as a sign of approval. This is a very small world. That hot FemDom you've had your eye on could have been somebody else's slave last year.

Trolling with Dignity

Trolling is the fisherman's term for trailing a baited line slowly in the water. Or, it can mean to search for something or someone. In our world, it is frequently a derogatory word for a method of linking up with a partner by running through every possible partner you can find.

Not that it's a bad idea, but you have to have a few rules while doing it. If I were a male submissive, I'd volunteer at the greetings desk of the local BDSM educational organization. That way, I'd see all the new lovely FemDoms, and they would see me.

You can also volunteer to be a DM (dungeon monitor or the person who is the final safety referee in a scene he's observing) at the next party. That is a position of respect, not to mention power. Many FemDoms, including me, prefer powerful men at their feet. Ladies like a gent who is willing to serve. It also absolves you from playing if you don't have a partner. If you don't have CPR training at this time, get it. Then, offer your services. Everyone will love you. FemDoms will notice you.

Act in a respectful manner and serve all who would wish it, not just the final candidates. A word of caution: don't serve anyone who currently has someone serving them. The other submissives can be very protective of their roles, as well as their Mistresses. Many are only submissive to that special Lady and think nothing of being aggressive should they feel the situation warrants it.

Try to develop a fellowship with other submissive gents or ladies, even if you normally don't join groups. They are your brothers and sisters on this journey. Their experience may be invaluable. In addition, if you prove to be a good friend, they may offer a reference that will earn you time with a Dominant Lady.

NETWORKING

It's okay if I:	Because I'll be advertising:
Serve soft drinks to everyone at the party, even the Alpha Males	Serving skills to potential Dommes and their friends
Volunteer to be a Security Guard or Dungeon Monitor at a party	That I am trusted and can take charge when necessary
Hold doors for ladies at work	I'm a gentleman

Reading the Ads Realistically

It's time to place an ad. Realistically, there are probably ten to twenty men online for every woman in the world of online dating. Many of those women appear to be professionals who want you to go to their pay website. You need to write an ad anyway.

You can use it as a beginning point for curious Ladies whom you have contacted. If the Lady discovers your ad, that's all the better.

You may wish to place an ad on websites such as www.bondage.com or www.collarme.com. There are many sites out there. Please choose one that is secure so others will not see your real name, offsite e-mail or address.

You don't fish for a shark in a swimming pool. Don't fish for a FemDom in a site in which they are not going to be accepted, or they must remain invisible. Although I've heard of exceptions, I do not suggest that you go to vanilla dating sites, such as www.eharmony.com, and expect to find the perfect Dominant Lady. I actually filled out their excruciatingly long application form only to find out they didn't think they would have anyone right for me. On their website, they stated they have 90 successful marriages a day. They couldn't match me up with anyone. I surmise it is because I am a Dominant female and filled out the questionnaire accordingly. Had I been a Dominant male, perhaps the problem would not exist, but I don't know.

Either way, I think you'll have better luck with the kink sites.
You may not, however. I hear gentlemen say they rarely have a Lady return their introductory e-mail. This may be true. However, it's good practice, and it gives you a forum to strut your stuff. If you are clear in what you can offer, it gives you the advantage of clear thought when the opportunity to meet the Lady arises.

As a courtesy, answer every inquiry to your ad, even if it's from the gay cross dresser who likes your photo and thinks you'd look great in fishnets. You never know when his best friend may be a Domme.

Peruse the ads of your competition. These are the males in your age range who share your interests, have a similar educational or cultural back-ground and enjoy the same kind of activities. Read their ads and decide what is attractive and what is a deterrent to getting a successful response or nibble. Successful car salesmen follow this approach; so can you.

To write an ad, use the tables you have completed and highlight the qualities and accomplishments you think may attract the Dominant Lady of your Dreams. Create a name that encompasses as many of those strong points as possible. It is perfectly acceptable to associate yourself with a favor-able image, whether it is Tarzan or Cary Grant. Just be sure to do it with a bit of humor and don't come across as a braggart. When picking an ad name, try to make it something she would like rather than something that makes you look good. Therefore, Foot Worshipper is better than Six Pack Stud, because it indicates what you are going to do for her, rather than focuses the attention on you.

Write an introduction in your own voice, putting your best foot forward. If you are a good-old-boy from the Georgia, you can sound like a southern gentleman. Avoid mysterious invitations that promise you'll divulge more information later. Sneaky is not a quality most of us are searching for. If you have a Scottish last name, but have never been out of the United States, avoid giving the impression you have a brogue, a snapshot of the Loch Ness Monster, or anything else she can see through in the second phone conversation. She has a bullshit meter, and she knows how to use it. Your goal is to get through her filter and stay solidly on the other side.

Once she understands a bit about who you are, and she has decided to read more of the ad, convey how you have been preparing to meet her. Check back in your journals and your resumé. It is easy to overlook something that is second nature to you, but would be highly desirable to the FemDom. Do not ramble. If it's a challenge, write your accomplishments in a list. State it as fact and not bragging. In other words, do not use more adjectives than necessary. Do not state weaknesses in the ad. When you do tell her about them, have a plan for remediation ready to execute before they become a problem.

The next paragraph of your ad concerns character. Refer to your previous charts and notes. You know who you are, and you want to give the impression that you are comfortable in your own skin. Indicate how your strong character will benefit her, if possible. Do not indicate character flaws. If you make it through her filters, you can introduce those later.

Declaring interests is always a bit of a problem. If you've fantasized about being kidnapped and brutalized by a Nazi interrogator, that's fine. Just don't put it in the ad. It's private, and when she has earned the right to know your deepest, darkest fantasies, you can share them with her. She may arrange the abduction for your birthday three years from now. However, you have to make it through her filters before she'll consider it. For right now, state your interests in a way that does not appear needy or demanding. Share interests that create a common ground, ones you hope both of you will enjoy.

The only time to declare interests that will reduce your appeal and subsequent number of favorable responses is when you absolutely have to have an element in the relationship. For example, if you require a substantial age difference for both play and service, and you know you aren't going to be able to tolerate a younger woman or one closer to your age, it is perfectly acceptable to state your preference. Expect fewer nibbles once you've added your own filter, but be satisfied that by narrowing the field earlier, you will not waste time. Frankly, you don't need eleven mistresses; you need one. If she likes your ad, or if she knows a friend who will, she may give you an introduction.

Close with a pitch. The entire ad could be considered a pitch. You are the salesman, and you are also the product you're selling. This is the last thing she will read before deciding whether or not to contact you. Validate who she is and why she should write. Avoid any negatives or passive words that sound wishy-washy or do not promote the positive energy you've generated.

Choose a photo that communicates what you want, but does not compromise your need for privacy. I usually use photos of my legs and feet, because I want to attract foot worshipping men. I do not use a head shot for family privacy. Do not, for any reason, take a picture of your erect penis and stick it in your ad. FemDoms know that a penis is a default on a male.

Use a spell checker as well as a grammar checker, even if you don't think they are important. Do not use capitals where they don't belong. Avoid exclamation points and double or triple punctuation, as in ???. You never know when the absolutely perfect FemDom is an English teacher.

Reread the entire ad aloud. Add transitions where it sounds disjointed. Is it professional without being sterile? Does it convey what you want to say? Take a moment to read the ad from the FemDom's point of view. What about your ad will attract her? What kind of woman will respond to your ad?

WRITING THE AD

Elements of an ad	Execution
Catchy name	Jeeves, at your service
Introduction	Good evening, Ma'am. Allow me to introduce myself. I'm Jeeves, and I serve ladies of quality and refinement.
Preparation	In preparation to serve you, I have completed courses in Italian cuisine, wine selection and table service. I study etiquette manuals and relationship books. In addition to being a handyman, I can keep house and manage laundry.
Character	I am a fiscally responsible single man who thrives on pleasing others. I appreciate clear directions, but do not require micromanaging. I enjoy meeting deadlines and learning new experiences.

Interests	Should the lady wish more than a service slave, I consider myself to be a masochist for impact play. Cock and ball torture and humiliation play are possibilities with the right lady. My specialty is orgasm play.
Pitch	
Photo	Serving at dinner in butler attire. Shot from the neck down.
Check for grammar	
Check for spelling	

If writing the ad is very difficult, or if it does not yield results, approach it from the opposite direction. Write the ad through the lady's point of view, advertising the Mistress who is hoping to attract you. It may give you a few hints on how to rewrite yours before putting it online.

Conclusion

Do the final edit on the ad and submit it. Congratulate yourself on doing the best job you could.

In this chapter you used all of the skills you have learned in the previous chapters to advertise yourself. You've learned how to present yourself to attract the kind of Dominant Lady about whom you have had fantasies. In addition, you've broadened your approach to finding that special someone.

Last, but not least, you have written an ad and sent it to a magazine, newspaper or website. What do you do until you get a response? You forget about it. Check the e-mail frequently, but do not place too much importance on the ad.   Most of the benefit came from writing it, which clarified your plan to capture a Mistress.

An M/s Studies Book

Chapter Nine
Close the Deal

Take a few minutes to review all you have accomplished. Revel in the fact that you are taking positive steps to capture a Mistress, not any FemDom, but the kind of quality lady of your dreams. She's out there, and she'll probably find you, or one of them will find you, when you least expect it. Very possibly, you will recognize her first, because you know exactly what you are looking for and you've expanded your vision to include real, live ladies. Therefore, it's important to stay prepared.

You wrote a resumé. Keep it updated as you add more and more accomplishments to your repertoire.

You are working on your appearance and how you present to others. You may wish to buy t-shirts with slogans that attract FemDoms like, "My genes aren't recessive; they're submissive." It's witty. I wrote it. It's yours. Make up more slogans and wear them proudly. Every minute of every day, you are advertising your product, which is you.

You are creating an online presence which will take some time to maintain and nurture. You can enter chat rooms and refer new friends to your online ad. You never know when the friend will match you with a Lovely Lady.

You are tracking your progress, either in the checklists in the Appendix or in a journal. You know when you are getting closer to your goals and when you are taking a break. You are beginning to exude the excitement of the chase. Most importantly, you are beginning to take risks.

People take risks when they can hold at bay the negative self-talk and the fears that keep them hostage, and realize that we are no different from them. However, with a plan, you are in more control, not of others and the situations, but of yourself, your perceptions, and your approach to the hunt.

What happens when a FemDom answers your ad or contacts you? What do you do? You respond using your good manners, and you read the book again, quickly. Frequently, the relationship will start with e-mail exchanges. Reread them, save them, and check them for spelling and grammar errors, even if hers aren't perfect. Go back and figure out how you could improve on e-mail exchanges next time.

First Meetings

Reread the book, but this time with the idea that you have a prospective Mistress and you want to encourage a vibrant relationship, whether it is short-term, long-term or a one-night stand. They are all perfect.

If you already do what is in the next several paragraphs, that's great. I include "dating" behavior, because too often males skip steps, and you only get one first impression.

Offer to meet her at a public place, either at a kink event or at a coffee shop. Make certain that both of you have safe calls, even if it's with volunteers from an online safe call organization in Timbuktu that you found on the Internet.

Do not invite her for a drink. Alcohol does goofy things to the power exchange dynamic, not to mention common sense and the ability to remember the conversation accurately.   For your safety, you don't want to remember the encounter very differently than she does. No alcohol the first time. There will be plenty of time to celebrate later.

She may wish to meet at her favorite restaurant, a public library, or some other venue that has several people nearby. If she does, accept her location.

If not, offer to choose a restaurant or coffee shop in a mutually convenient location that has a security camera, for both your safety and hers. Become familiar with the establishment, the menu, and the driving directions so you can arrive ten minutes early and get a table or claim the reservation. Do not order until she arrives. Negotiate beforehand whether this is coffee, dessert or a "date" for a full meal. If you were expecting a steak dinner, and she only wants a piece of pie, you both order pie, regardless of what she says.

I adore having lunch with gentlemen. I also need to watch my weight, so I negotiate ahead of time to split a dinner. Do not offer that option, but respond in the affirmative if she asks. Actually, respond in the affirmative to pretty much anything that you can wrap your head around without sacrificing your ethics or your dietary restrictions. Initially, she's looking for a gentleman who can be part of her team, not necessarily the other way around.

Rise when she enters. Seat her. Don't talk too much or ask personal questions. Act interested and be interesting, even if you have to pre-screen your topics. Discuss kink when she brings it up. Answer her questions truthfully, without giving too much information. You can bear your soul after the deal is closed. If the Lady tells you she must leave at a certain time, set your cell phone alarm for five minutes before the deadline and facilitate her leaving. Try to gauge the meeting to end slightly before she feels it should. Make certain by stating it clearly, if it's true, that you would like to see her again, and that you appreciate the time she elected to spend with you.

Pick up the check, even if she offers to split it with you. Later, after your relationship is a little more stable, you can negotiate finances. If this is the last time you meet, you'll have been perceived as a gentleman of quality, and even though you two may not hit it off, she may know the perfect lady to invite to coffee next week.

Within a few hours of arriving home, write an e-mail thanking her. Try to get that e-mail to her before she has a chance to send one of her own. If you know her address, and you know her real name, and that it is okay to receive mail, a card is appropriate. Should you wish to create a signature move, send a single red rose or small gift. It conveys your gratitude that she chose to spend time with you. Do not spend much on the gift, because you are going to send the same thing to every FemDom after the first meeting. This is a very small community, and we talk. The last thing you want is for us to become jealous of each other, because our friendships are frequently stronger than our desire to grant an audience to a male.

Continue an e-mail and casual relationship until she gives you signals that she wants something more, and it meets your needs to ask her for a play date or to offer her a petition.

Play Dates

Play dates are natural outcomes of your growing relationship that are based on the Kinky Play discussed earlier in the book. Once you have established a basic relationship, you can explore the activities you both like.

The exception is the one-night stand at a play party at a kink event. You are in public, so security is not a problem. A play party usually has people, called dungeon monitors or DMs, who are not playing, but are supervising the play and evaluating safety issues. However, you may want to check out her references before you let her hang a bowling ball from your private parts.

After the type of Kinky Play is selected, and the activities determined, it is important to discuss the type and level of Power Exchange until an agreement has been met. At a play party, there may not be an elaborate power exchange. In private, you have much more freedom and time to create the fantasy.

At this point, you have a kinky activity or activities and a level of power exchange, so now you need to select a time and place. I recommend a kinky play party over a private session, but it is your choice. Use safe calls. Be on time. Help set up beforehand and clean up afterward. Although you may need aftercare, the nurturing time following a scene, be aware that she, too, may need some of that kind of attention.

Send an e-mail thanking her, and if you have established a signature move, send it. What you send after a play date can be different from your choice for the first meeting, in part because there could be a lot of play dates, but there is only one first meeting. Something as simple as a gourmet chocolate presented after a play date or scene suffices.

Debrief within three days and be honest, truthful and gentle. This is a good activity for a phone call. Sometimes FemDoms are a little uncomfortable with what we do to men. She may appreciate reassurance. If you liked it, say so. If you didn't, measure her pleasure against your honesty. If you couldn't stand it, make it a hard no for next time. Thank her for the time she chose to spend with you.

When your play dates are considered a success, and you know you want a relationship that involves a stronger commitment, offer a petition.

Petitions

A petition is a request. Since you are making it, you have to figure out what you want and how you will know if she has granted you what you have asked. This isn't really a negotiation. It's a plea. She doesn't have to acknowledge it, although that is somewhat rude not to.

Many men start out with this step in the first five minutes of discovering the FemDom and are amazed at the complete lack of response they get. Don't petition anyone for anything unless you have done the groundwork to close the sale. In other words, develop a relationship that is worth keeping before offering your petition. It's like selling a book to a publisher. Offer one at a time.

Too often, Ladies of Dominance receive petitions too early to consider them seriously, and the male will probably not offer twice. Wait until there appears to be a need beyond the casual encounter. Wait until you perceive that both of you want to increase the level of power exchange. Petitions are all about power exchange. Be sure that is what you request of the Lady before asking.

There is no one right way to ask a Lady for more of her time, more of her attention, and a stronger commitment. Try to state what you feel for her, what she does that makes you a better person, and how you wish to serve. Be succinct in how she benefits from the union. Do not put time allotments, contracts or ultimatums in the petition. All factors can be negotiated once she decides she wants you in her life.

Do not petition for anything you can't deliver. Only petition for what is viable and does not take away from the commitments you have already made in your life.

The answer to a successful petition is "yes". That's it. Request what will yield that response. Do not hide a request you know she won't like very well behind ones you know she needs. Once you have petitioned and received an affirmative, you can discuss the details of what that commitment entails and its duration. Celebrate the moment when she accepts.

Contracts

Kinky contracts are exactly what they are in the mundane world, except they are not legally binding. Two people agree on what they will do, when and where they will do it, how they will do it, and what happens when one of the parties doesn't keep the commitment. Contracts do not cover why two people are doing it, although that is a viable point of discussion prior to signing one. Unlike petitions, which are composed exclusively by you, contracts are created by both parties.

There are plenty of examples of contracts out there on the Internet. I suggest you and your Lady write your own based on your particular situation rather than selecting a template. Write a contract when you need a contract and not before. If one of you needs a contract, consider that both of you need one to support the relationship. Write the contract to meet the least demanding requests that are common to both parties.

Choose dates of short duration on the first contract. It is better to end a relationship after a contract has run out than to break one, which is bad form and indicates a lack of dedication or realism necessary to making the relationship work. Contracts can be for an evening, a weekend, or a lifetime. I recommend a three-month contract if you think this is the Lady of your Dreams.

Create a brief break between the last date of the first contract and the first date of the next one to be used for renegotiation. The next contract should reflect the changes that have occurred in your relationship.

Collars

A collar differs from a contract in that a contract describes behavior and a collar does not. A collar is a token of a state of commitment between the Mistress (choose your own title) and the slave, puppy, or submissive, and does not denote what actually happens in the relationship. Contracts determine that, and although many long-term kinksters do not use them, I recommend their use, at least in the beginning stages of a relationship. Some couples combine a verbal contract with the collar, but I do not recommend verbal contracts, because people forget what they said.

Collars are different from petitions or contracts. The petition is offered by you, the contract is agreed upon by both, but the collar is offered by the FemDom. You do not control when a collar is offered or its parameters. You do control whether or not you agree to accept the collar she has offered. If the relationship is severed, the collar is returned to the Mistress.

There are as many collars out there as couples or families that use them. Each collar can be tailored to the needs of the FemDom and her slave. If he needs to practice discretion, the wide, locked, leather collar with the D-ring in the front is not going to fly under the radar of the vanilla people who will not understand the commitment.

The collar can be a piece of jewelry, such as my slave's pocket watch, or an item of clothing, such as a handkerchief. Wearing it keeps the slave in focus and mindful of the commitment to his Owner.

Different collars serve different purposes, and most are designed for short-term use. A **collar of protection** is one usually offered for a specific time period and assists the submissive by safely introducing him to the kink community. A **guardianship** is a newer kind of collar that provides an uncollared slave a Dominant or a family until he finds a more permanent one. It is based on a power exchange relationship and is expected to be temporary. A **temporary collar** is offered for a discreet period of time, such as a weekend, for a relationship that is not originally designed to be permanent. A **training collar** is offered by a Domme for specific reasons, such as teaching a new skill to a slave or guiding him along his path of submission.

A **collar of consideration** is offered when the FemDom believes she might want you in her family forever and wants a trial period before making a decision. A **permanent collar** is awarded to you when she commits to you for a lifetime, which is as close to marriage as we get in the kink community.

An **online collar** can be temporary or permanent. To separate FemDoms from male slaves, the slave writes his name and adds his Mistress's name in brackets at the end, such as luckyboy[Destiny] or luckyboy{D}. He writes his name and the pronoun I in lower case.

There is plenty of time in a relationship for collars, and I do not recommend jumping into one hastily. You have all the time in the world.

There you have it, the nuts and bolts of remaking yourself into the gentleman who will attract the Lady of his Dreams. I have given you some tools, but, Dear Reader, it is your responsibility to take action.

Now, go capture a Mistress.

An M/s Studies Book

Appendix A

CHARACTERISTICS OF A DOMINANT LADY

Characteristic	Evidence in Behavior

Appendix B

FANTASY AND REALITY

Fantasy	Need	Reality

Appendix C

SERVICE PRACTICE

Service	Date	Person	Location	Comments

Appendix D

COMMUNICATION SKILLS

Skill	Level of Expertise with Dominant Ladies	What am I going to do about it?

Appendix E

STRENGTHS

Strength	Why is it an asset?	How can I use it?	How can I advertise it?	Who will want it?
Trait:				
Skill:				
Accomplishment:				
To please her:				

Appendix F

WEAKNESSES

Weakness	Why is it a weakness?	What will I do about it?	By when?	How will I let her know I'm working on it?
Trait:				
Skill:				
Ashamed:				
Not pleasing Mistress:				

SITUATION

Situation	Why could it be a problem?	What can I do to minimize it?	When do I tell her?
Health:			
Family:			
Time:			
Money:			

Appendix G

GROWTH PLAN

Objective	Plan	Evaluation
I will improve:		
I will improve:		
I will improve:		
I will improve:		
I will improve:		
I will improve:		
I will improve:		
I will improve:		
I will improve:		
I will improve:		

Appendix H

SKILLS

Skills I possess	Where can I show it off in the kink world?	Where can I show it off in the vanilla world?

IMPROVING PERCEPTIONS

Narrow perceptions that I can broaden	How can I broaden them?

Appendix I

Fill in the blanks to help you understand the relationship between how you look and how you feel:

I like to wear _____, because it makes me feel _____. The Lady I want to attract will see me and think _____. I like her to wear _____, because it makes me feel _____. I can serve her when she wears it, because _____.

IMPRESSIONS

I want her to see me as (a):	So, I will wear:	Do I currently own what I need?	Where and how will I get it?

Appendix J

CREATING A NICHE MARKET

My niche, even if I don't know much now	What I need to learn	How I can demonstrate mastery

SKILLS AND ADVERTISING

Skills worth advertising	The skill makes me feel:	Projecting the image

Appendix K

SOLUTIONS TO LIMITATIONS

I can't:	Therefore I will:	And it will be perceived that:

CREATE A LIFE ONLINE

In real life, I'm:	But online, I could be:	So:

Appendix L

NETWORKING

It's okay if I:	Because I'll:

Appendix M

WRITING THE AD

Elements of an ad	Execution
Catchy name	
Introduction	
Preparation	
Character	
Interests	
Pitch	
Photo	
Check for grammar	
Check for spelling	

An M/s Studies Book

About the Author

In her non-kink world, Karen Martin is a retired educator whose graduate degree is in speech pathology. That's not as interesting as her kink resumé. In her kink life, Karen's scene name is Brenna and she is a FemDom who has owned a male slave since the spring of 2002. She was accepted into the Austin Mentors Program in 2003 where she expanded her knowledge of the art of dominance. She has served both as the education director for SAADE (School for Advanced American Dominant Education) and as a SAADE Council Member – an appointed position based on merit.

Currently, Karen serves as the acquisitions editor for The Nazca Plains Corporation, the largest publisher of BDSM in the US. In that position, she searches for new authors who can bring original and fascinating material to the kink community.

For her own amusement, Karen plays "Miss Brenna," Brenna5461, a phone dominatrix on Nightflirt (www.nightflirt.com). This is the playground where she flexes her psychological muscles and creates lovely Victorian dungeons in the minds of those precious gentlemen who call her.

Made in the USA